CHANGE YOUR GAME, CHANGE YOUR LIFE

HOW A SIMPLE SHIFT IN FOCUS WILL COMPLETELY TRANSFORM YOUR RELATIONSHIP TO GOLF… AND EVERYTHING ELSE!

<u>CHANGE YOUR GAME,</u>
<u>CHANGE YOUR LIFE</u>

HOW A SIMPLE SHIFT IN FOCUS WILL COMPLETELY
TRANSFORM YOUR RELATIONSHIP TO GOLF…
AND EVERYTHING ELSE!

Andrew McKee

Change Your Game, Change Your Life: How a simple shift in focus will completely transform your relationship to golf — And everything else!

Edited by Kathy Chandler
Cover Art by Stefanie Nickolaisen
Interior Graphics by Gheen Hillman

You can contact author at:

www.changeyourgamechangeyourlife.com

andrew@whatsmycontact.com

ISBN-10: 099688520X
ISBN-13: 978-0-9968852-0-1

Library of Congress Control Number 2015916090

First Edition

To My Dad and Steve Chandler
The two most influential men in my life.

Table of Contents

The Greatest Evidence of the
  Power of The Concept 1

1. Understanding "The Why" 7

2. The Beginning...15

3. How I Got Here 19

4. The Downward Spiral 29

5. Separation Anxiety 39

6. The Epiphany 45

7. The Concept 53

8. Barriers to Application 67

9. This Is as Technical as I Will Get 79

10. Five Things 91

11. The Case against Caring 97

12. Mushrooms and Dandelions..........................111

13. Don't Trust. LOVE! 119

14. Watch Your Language 127

15. It's All Thought 139

16. Health and Awareness.................................149

17. Commitment and Certainty 157

18. Moving the Baseline 165

19. The 19th Hole; What is YOUR Contact? 171

Why Capture My Message in a Book?....................179

Acknowledgments

Several people were both directly and indirectly (meaning that, until they read this, they may not have known) instrumental and inspirational in the completion of this book. Without their help and unwavering support and encouragement, my message would have remained inside me.

Steve Chandler
Byron Katie
Retief Goosen
P. James McKee (my dad)
Beverly McKee (my mom)
Jill McKee (my wife)
My Children
Mark Wahl
Vanessa Horn
Steve Tefsky
Christopher Dorris
Dusan Djukich
Matt Scott
Alan Bush

"90% OF ALL GOLFERS *NEVER* SEE THE CLUB HIT THE BALL."

WHY?

THIS BOOK CONTAINS THE ANSWER TO THAT QUESTION.

Introduction

The Greatest Evidence of the Power of The Concept

Have you ever had an idea that consumed your thoughts constantly and cried from inside you to get out?

Do you have something like that now? An idea you know would make a powerful difference in the lives of those who heard and embraced it? Is it something that is so meaningful to you that you feel compelled to share it, but can't seem to bring yourself to because of some seemingly insurmountable obstacles blocking your way?

Do you often lay awake at night with your mind spinning having so much energy around your thoughts that sleep refuses to overtake you?

If you have, or if you do now, I want you to know that I UNDERSTAND YOU!

I have just described the state that has been my very existence for the three years.

THE CONCEPT, as referred to in the title of this introduction, is the name I have given to the principle described in this book.

Without me grasping and applying this principle (which is the entire message of this book,) this book would not exist.

If the ONLY thing I accomplish in writing this book IS the writing and COMPLETION of it, it is more than enough!

You see, for as long as I remember, I have had an enormously challenging time completing tasks. I've always been a great starter and I've started lots of things that could have been great.

My childhood drawing pads are filled with elaborate pictures of dragons and hockey players who are carefully drawn in every detail until something on them was obviously just too hard for me to draw. Quite often, it was feet that would shut down my artistry. I just couldn't make feet look good enough to meet my standards of excellence.

Progression through school taught me there were other things that ought to be finished. I didn't do particularly well with those, either.

I performed very well on tests and would have cruised through my academic years with flying colors if I could just have eliminated those pesky assignments.

Somehow, I managed to graduate high school with decent enough grades and eventually went on to college, where multiple choice testing allowed me to achieve a respectable level of success.

As a matter of fact, I was well on my way to graduating with my bachelor's in business administration until MCOM 320 came along.

For those of you not familiar with it, MCOM 320 is the technical writing course everyone MUST pass in order to graduate from business school.

The problem with this class, and there really was only one problem, was that the final was not a test. It was an assignment. It was a HUGE assignment!

To complete the course work for MCOM 320, every student must turn in a final paper and that paper has to be at least 30 PAGES long!

Sorry. That just didn't work for me. I entered the last week of class—the first time I took it—with an A grade. I didn't turn in the paper. I couldn't do it. So, I took the class again the next semester.

This time I did the paper but didn't turn it in. I was sure it was terrible and that I hadn't fulfilled all the requirements to get a good grade on it. I failed the class for the second time.

The next semester (I was now running out of teachers to take the class from because I had to avoid the ones I had previously let down...) produced the same result. I had a great grade going in to the last week of school—of course I did, I had already taken the class twice! —but I just couldn't finish that paper. The biggest problem with this is that I was (supposedly) graduating!

My parents had flown in from 3000 miles away to see me walk across the stage in my cap and gown. Almost all of my friends had job offers they were moving on to.

You get the picture. And it was not a pretty one.

My teacher graciously extended the date for me to turn in my final college assignment until the week after I had unofficially graduated.

I went back to my apartment and sat down at the computer. I put every bit of mental energy I could into finishing that paper!

It wasn't enough. I didn't finish it. I didn't turn it in. I didn't really graduate.

I returned home from school with everyone believing I had a degree from a respected university. I carried around an enormous weight of guilt. I was a failure.

I had gone to college for almost seven years (Yes, even Tommy Boy was better than I was!) and I had nothing to show for it but some debt and a severely damaged self-esteem.

I probably would have gone to my grave without actually graduating had it not been for an opportunity that arose two years later that REQUIRED a college degree.

This time would be different. I retook the class for a fourth time through correspondence and finished the final paper at the absolute deadline!

The file from that class is the only file I have kept from college. The teacher told me I should consider writing as a career! Ha! That was fifteen years ago and, until I started working on this book, during those fifteen years I haven't written anything longer than an email.

What I have shared in this book is THE PRINCIPLE that has allowed me to remove the weight of shame that has been crushing my spirit most of my life!

I am now free to love what I am doing and to feel free and relaxed as I do it!

This has been nothing short of miraculous for me and I am filled with a desire to share what I have experienced with any and all who will hear!

I have written a book! I have shared it with the world! The world may receive it, as it will! Whether people like this book or not, THE MESSAGE contained in it is undeniably powerful! How do I know that? I know it because I was changed by it when I thought myself unchangeable.

Hello life. Welcome to Part II!

"SIMPLICITY IS THE ULTIMATE
SOPHISTICATION."

CLARE BOOTHE LUCE

Chapter 1

Understanding "The Why"

There is a WHY underlying everything you do in your life.

You don't have to understand this WHY. You don't. However, understanding the true WHY will almost always have the effect of changing behavior and results exponentially faster than not understanding.

If that sentence is confusing to you, be patient. It will make perfect sense to you by the time you finish this book and likely long before that.

As I get older, I become more convinced that children are correct in their relentless pursuit of knowing the answer to the question, WHY? They always want to know why and they aren't satisfied until they get to the real answer.

As adults, we seem to spend much of our time killing this instinct in our children so they will stop asking. I suppose there are a few reasons for not wanting to get asked the question WHY? The most obvious to me is that I don't know the answer.

What is keeping me from answering The Why or at least attempting to answer it? Could it be that I am too impatient to really get involved in seeking truth? Could it be that I don't want the answer because I'm afraid I won't like it? Or maybe I am not confident in my intellectual capacity to comprehend? No, really, WHY?

Imagine that you haven't been feeling well for some time. You have been tired and lethargic. You have had difficulty breathing and you feel a constant pain in your chest. Now imagine that you visit a doctor who, in an impatient pursuit of just giving you answers that will satisfy you and get you out of the office so that he can move on to the next patient, tells you to take caffeine pills every day and use an inhaler, and your problem will be solved.

Will that make you happy? Or would you rather know the true reason that you feel terrible and have help with alleviating that?

Caffeine pills and an inhaler might temporarily deal with the surface issues of being tired and struggling with breathing, but the underlying issue of that actual medical problem would be advancing unchecked and could ultimately create problems too great to overcome with Band-Aids and quick fixes.

Of course, it may seem ridiculous to suppose that a doctor would do such a thing, as his career is actually based on being able to answer the question.

I find, however, that in my own life I continually try to force things to work that are not working, without spending so much as a moment trying to come up with the actual reason WHY they are not working. I think most people can identify with me in this, as there is even a popular saying that summarizes this behavior.

"The definition of insanity is doing the same thing over and over and expecting different results."

The "WHY" I am referring to in the case of this book is contained in the quote on the title page. WHY do almost all amateur golfers fail to see the club hit the ball when they make contact with it and WHY does it matter? If this question can be answered effectively, it will be like stumbling upon the Holy Grail of golf wisdom. Well, come along. Let us ride to Camelot!

An Invitation to an Open Mind

Let me start by saying that this, at its core, is a golf book. A golf book intended to create change in the golf experience and performance of its readers by providing insight.

Few things (if any at all) bring me more delight and satisfaction than helping someone hit shots they have never hit before and seeing them become filled with hope because they have (finally!) found something that will improve their game! I cannot overstate the reward that comes from helping golfers shift their minds in a way that creates results and experiences that, in their previous state, could not have occurred.

Anyone who has taught the game of golf and had people benefit from their teaching understands this feeling of mutual accomplishment. I have found that golfers appreciate these "discoveries" and become as enthusiastic as religious zealots and political advocates in their sharing of them. Unfortunately, this is where the trouble can begin, as much of correct principles—particularly technical principles—gets lost somewhere between where the pro taught them and where the amateur is attempting to share them!

One method of creating a golf swing and game from the ground up is to work through years of methodical coaching and practice and become very proficient. This method will require dedication and perseverance, coupled with extensive swing analysis, professional instruction, and practice beyond that which most humans are willing to commit to anything in their lives.

It will cost thousands and thousands of dollars in monetary investment and even more in time investment. It will leave many frustrated to the point of mental exhaustion and frequently bring them to the brink of giving up. It can suck much of the enjoyment out of what otherwise could be a fantastic game. And it can give credence to Mark Twain's humorous commentary on golf, which he allegedly referred to as "A Good Walk, Spoiled."

This is, however, merely one option that can create some fantastic results for the few who are willing to commit to it and persevere. (They are called Pro Golfers!)

There is at least one other option.

I invite you to read this book with an open mind. Let me state that I do not consider its contents to be "The Way," in that its teachings are superior to all other teaching. What I will share with you in this book is an awakening I had that changed the relationship I had with golf and, as you will find, with most other things in my life.

What occurred for me was a change in mindset and perception. I will refer to this epiphany and the subsequent awakening that I experienced in the simplest manner I can throughout this book and in my coaching. To me, it is simply, "The Concept."

The Concept may not be original WITH me, but it is original TO me in the way I experienced it. This book is a collection of thoughts and observations that will begin with a bit of my own history as a golfer and continue along the journey that I have taken which has led me to where I am today.

I consider The Concept to be a foundational thought. To borrow a phrase from 3M:

This isn't your golf swing; this is what makes your golf swing work.

The Concept can most easily be compared to an operating system for your computer. If the operating system is installed and functioning properly, the programs you use will work effectively. If the operating system is faulty or not present, programs that would otherwise have fantastic capabilities will be useless to you.

The Concept provides an operating system, or foundational mindset, upon which all golf instruction may rest and function effectively, thereby providing the most value to you as the user. Simply put, this mind shift can have the effect of having your technical training work for you.

I believe that all golfers, when armed with this very simple concept, give themselves a foundation, or operating system, on top of which they may add the technicalities of professional golf training and other programs, to enhance and improve the experience of golf for them.

My view (based on experience) is that this concept is foundationally and fundamentally imperative to create an environment where all further teaching can be effective, efficient, and beneficial to you and bring joy to your experience of golf. Ultimately, isn't it joy that we really want from golf, anyway?

I want to create a setting in which you can most easily understand and internalize the fundamental idea contained in this book. To do so, I will start at the beginning and lead you on a very condensed journey from my first childhood exposure to golf to my present day. I will share with you some very dramatic experiences that have let to a complete evolution of my relationship with golf.

I will attempt to do this in the simplest way possible, adding only the information I believe will add to the value of The Concept for you. I have learned that having things in their simplest form is always the best for me.

This is what I do in my coaching. The most effective coaching and teaching is created from SIMPLICITY and REPETITION. Let me say that again: SIMPLICITY and REPETITION.

You will notice lots of Simplicity and Repetition in the pages that follow!

What you think is the problem with your golf game, isn't. The true "problems" lie in things that most people have never thought of and never will without help.

Chapter 2

The Beginning

Before writing this book, I searched every source I could think of for something that would teach what I wanted to communicate in the way I wanted it communicated.

Not only could I not find a book or magazine that filled my wishes, I couldn't find anything close. That left me with only one option: I had to write it down and share it.

I started off by writing down a few thoughts and insights and planned on giving those out in a pamphlet or tract, but as I wrote, I realized that the true impact of what I wanted to share could never be conveyed in a two or three-page publication. It would require detailed explanation, clarification, stories, experiences, and supporting evidence.

The power of The Concept was something I yearned to have my family, friends, and future friends discover for themselves. And creating an environment in which this discovery could take place would require much more energy and effort from me than just a couple of hours of work writing down a few lines about an experience I had. It would require me doing something I had never done before and never imagined I could do.

The fact that you are reading this now means that I did it.

The discovery I am about to explain to you, in the best way I can with the written word, has been GROUNDBREAKING for me in golf. Not only has it restored my love of the game, but it has also taken both my love of the game and my ability to play it to an entirely new level!

If an increased love for the game of golf and a greater ability to play it is something you wish to experience for yourself, then I wholeheartedly invite you to continue reading!

I find psychology to be the most fascinating element of sports. This is likely due to the fact that, even though I had a respectable level of physical skill for many sports, I found over years of participation and competition that my mental fortitude was lacking and consistently held me back.

Golf, of all sports, exists more in the head than it does in the body and therefore, anyone who plays golf should find more benefit to their game from improving their mental approach than from anything they could do physically.

It is also important for me to say that The Concept I present in this book may NOT benefit all golfers. Not all golfers will have the ability to embrace it. It will fly in the face of the beliefs and teachings of many of the world's greatest and many of the world's worst golfers (who will mostly remain in that category because of their inability to admit that they don't know everything).

For example, I'm not certain Tiger Woods (of course, he would be the one I would choose) would receive much benefit from meeting with me to discuss my approach because he has not shown (from my viewpoint, inaccurate as it may be, given that I don't actually know him) a great willingness to receive any mental coaching. He does, however, seem more than willing to expend massive amounts of time, energy, and money tinkering with the technicalities of his golf "swing."

But I don't believe Tiger's swing is the problem with his game. It never has been.

It's his mental game that has been decimated since his very public personal struggles, and it's his pride that will keep him from being able to overcome it. I don't judge him. I would quite possibly do the same if I were in his orthopedic shoes. (That is a not-so-veiled reference to the new style of golf shoe he is wearing as I write this book, that make him look as though he's late for his shift at the hospital.)

Tiger's physical skills are still superior to basically every golfer on the planet but his mind doesn't seem to be right. He tries to do too much. He is too wrapped up in the technical aspect of his swing. No, his swing is not his problem.

For most amateurs, "the swing" is not the problem either, even in cases where their swings are atrocious.

When you work with the mind, the body follows. That is why everyone who works with me finds that their swing changes, and in some cases very drastically, without spending so much as five minutes on anything technical.

The great discovery is that The Concept shines the light of clarity on things that most golfers perceive as root problems in their "golf swings." The things they are seeing as "roots" are actually branches.

More clearly stated:

What you think is the problem with your golf game, isn't. The Concept will show you the real sources of trouble. The true "problems" lie in things that most people have never thought of and never will without help.

That having been said, let us proceed.

"YOU CAN DISCOVER MORE ABOUT A PERSON IN AN HOUR OF PLAY THAN IN A YEAR OF CONVERSATION."

PLATO

Chapter 3

How I Got Here

I began playing golf around the age of twelve.

My father has golfed for at least 40 years and still loves to get out on the course to walk in nature, see the birds (one of his greatest sources of joy and the source of much terror for the family, as he also frequently tries to spot them while driving — but that's another story) and get away from the stresses of everyday life.

I was absolutely thrilled to get my first set of clubs as a gift from him. The clubs were Haig Ultras with light blue grips that were actually ladies' clubs that were short enough for me to play with.

They were very nice and far more expensive than anything I should have gotten at the time, as our family was really struggling financially. But my dad, who always wanted to provide the best for his children, asked me if I would take care of them and appreciate them and said if I would, he would buy them for me.

I promised him that I would. I kept that promise for a number of years until accidently throwing my driver into the middle of the lake at our cottage in the beautiful country of northern Ontario. That's a story for a different time.

I still have the rest of those clubs and my son plays with them now.

From the day I first played a round with my dad on our little par-3 course with those sparkling women's blades, I became taken with the desire to beat him.

My self-esteem seemed to be partially, if not entirely, connected to beating my father at golf. I would come close many times, but would be unable to close the deal.

The most memorable of these close calls came when I was 14 or 15 years old and was having the round of my life. I want to paint as clear a picture of this as I can, as it really is the central experience of the next few chapters of this book.

Heading into the 16th hole on a course that we had played many times together, I was ahead of my dad by four shots and was brimming with confidence, as this particular hole set up perfectly for me.

There was a creek that meandered its way through the course and ran along the left side of this hole. The edge of the creek was lined with tall, leafy trees that made it impossible to see the green from the tee box, as the hole dog-legged to the left where the creek took a 90-degree turn. The hole measured around 350 yards, but was actually only about 290 if you cut the corner and went straight at it by flying the ball over the trees.

I could hit the ball quite far and very high and always attempted this route. Choosing the risky line would often cost me a penalty stroke or two, but not that day. No. That day I flushed one (quite rare) and watched with eager anticipation as the ball seemed to travel in slow motion, outlined against the blue, cloudless, Canadian sky (also rare) and easily carried over the trouble on a perfect line right at the green!

I was so excited, I could barely wait for my dad to hit his shot so I could go up and find what was certainly the best drive I had ever hit on that hole. This would most certainly put the final nail in the coffin, as I was about to finally beat my dad.

I was not at all worried when he hit his ball out into the middle of the fairway, leaving himself just over a hundred yards to the green. I practically ran up to the green to apply a little "gamesmanship" pressure to Dad as I located my ball just off the fringe no more than twenty feet from the flag! Victory was mine! All I had left was an easy chip that I could possibly hole-out for eagle but would certainly knock up to a couple of feet for birdie!

I stood impatiently by my ball waiting for dad to hit his shot so that the round could be over with and a new order of supremacy — the rightful order — established. After this, the only holes remaining were a simple straightforward par 4 with no trouble and an easy par-three, which presented no real challenge to me and would make it virtually impossible for Dad to make up a four or five shot deficit.

Such were the thoughts that were running through my triumphant teenage mind as my dad addressed his ball 120 yards from the green.

He looked so small and hopeless out there so far away from the tiny green. Without so much as a practice swing — he never takes one — he took the club back and then swung, and the ball took flight.

The next three seconds occurred differently for me than any previous passage of time had in my life. I gazed in horror as my dad's golf ball flew majestically through the air on a perfect, high arc, landed softly on the front of the green, took one bounce and began tracking, as if guided by some sort of fatalistic homing beacon, straight into the flag and dropped in the cup. An eagle two!

ARE YOU KIDDING ME?!!!!

My lungs instantly deflated as though a 500-pound sumo wrestler had just body-slammed me to the canvas.

There are a precious few experiences in my life that have had such power that they literally remained with me to the point where I can relive them in my mind whenever and wherever I choose. And this one is right at the forefront of all of those memorable experiences.

Whatever belief I had built up in myself through practice and effort immediately vanished and I knew without question that I would never beat my dad at golf as long as I lived!

Somewhat less consciously, my self-esteem took a severe lashing and become stunted in its progress. I literally felt like I was less of a person, less worthy of anything good that may otherwise have found its way into my life through cosmic channels.

I struggled to finish out the hole, chunking my chip shot and then three-putting for bogey to find myself on the losing end of the rarely-to-be-experienced three-shot-swing.

You can well guess what followed. I bogeyed the simple par 4 17th and dropped another shot. That made four dropped shots in the last two holes.

In my deflated state I plodded across the road to the par 3 as my father most certainly still chuckled and chortled over one of the most miraculous shots he had ever hit.

Looking back, I should have found it inside myself to celebrate a little with him. I mean, it was an amazing shot and there is no question that my golfing that day was a gift from my dad and likely a bit of a financial stretch for us during that period in our family's lives. A little gratitude and happiness for him would have been nice, and certainly deserved.

Unfortunately, my mind at that point of my development was unable to see the bright side and was resigned to what immediately followed. I went on to bogey the par 3 and watch my dad birdie as my fate was sealed and I lost by one shot.

It was over.

It would be several more years before I could contend on a regular basis. I found, in retrospect, that the relationship I created with my father in golf would be the relationship that I would have with basically every person I would play golf with from that time forward. Only one thing would matter to me: Winning.

My self-worth was literally dependent upon it.

Having your self-esteem dependent upon how well you hit a golf ball is no way to go through life.

Of course, because I spent an enormous amount of time doing it, I did continue to develop as a golfer. Eventually, my dad could not keep up with my length and I did start to beat him on a regular basis. That didn't, however, seem to lessen the devastation I felt that day; I'm not sure I ever recovered from that loss until just recently.

Upon reading this, my dad did offer the apology that should have been extended years ago. Thanks, Dad. I appreciate it.

Those early years playing with my father seemed to establish a pattern for my golfing. I always wanted to play but that want was always driven by a desire to beat whomever I was playing with. I got good enough that I usually would beat whomever I was out with, including anyone who joined up with us to fill out a foursome. Please keep in mind, however, that I grew up in Canada and the golf season there is unreasonably short, and therefore does not produce a high number of really good golfers.

*   *   *

Many years ago when I was still in my late twenties, I played a round of golf with my uncle Al. Uncle Al is a spectacular human and I have always greatly respected his opinions. He is one of a few people in life who is so emotionally steady and even-keeled that nothing seems to upset or bother him. That quality makes him lots of fun to be around and an absolute pleasure to play golf with.

We were playing a really nice course that day and got matched up with a 19-year-old kid who worked there and played on his days off.

I struggled around the golf course, managing to save par from several difficult circumstances. I hit a few good shots and some big drives, but also managed to visit several bushes and a lake or two. Anyway, I ground my way through the round and as we walked off the course and tallied up the scores I found that I had shot 79, which was exactly the same as our guest had scored.

Well, in a poorly-veiled attempt to receive some sort of validation and verify that my uncle was impressed with what I had accomplished, I asked Al whether he thought I or this other kid was a better golfer. His answer was something that has remained with me for years and triggered a change in my life that would start me down the path to what I believe was enlightenment.

He said, diplomatically (as always) and without hesitation, "You know you're probably about equal as golfers; it just looks like you're working a lot harder."

This was not the compliment I was looking for.

Little did Al know what kind of an impact that statement would have in my life. I took it rather personally and decided that I would prove to him (and everyone else, for that matter) over the course of the next little while that I could make golf look as easy for me as it did for that teenager.

I sought the advice of a golf professional and began taking lessons. This is where I was exposed for the first time in my life to what my swing looked like on video. Wow. It was depressing.

It's amazing how easily and clearly this relates to how I often view myself in other aspects of my life. My perception of what I look like doing things in life is most likely very different from the reality. It certainly was with my golf swing.

This was probably my first realization that who I thought I was and who I actually was were quite different.

Anyway, without getting too metaphysical, I want to return to what showed up on the video. What I saw was someone working very hard to try to produce a certain result with a very ugly golf swing; not at all the swing I thought I had.

Hitting the ball a long way was very important to my ego and me and to make sure I accomplished it, I was putting everything I could into each and every swing.

It showed.

Although it wasn't a pretty swing, it was functional and when my timing was on I could get a decent amount of good golf out of it. When my timing was off, however, I was a disaster waiting to happen.

It turns out the wait for this disaster was about twenty years, but happen it did!

"IT IS BY CHOICE AND NOT BY CHANCES THAT WE CHANGE OUR CIRCUMSTANCES."

NADIA SAHARI

Chapter 4

The Downward Spiral

Reflecting back, I now see that the actual descent to where I lost the love for the game of golf began the day I first picked up a club.

A series of unfortunate events and unpleasant experiences where I lost my cool, interspersed with minor triumphs and moments of happiness, led me to where I was a few months before I started writing this book.

I will share a couple of the lowlights with you to give you some insight into how severe the problem had gotten with me.

Of course, there is the obligatory "throwing" of the golf club from time to time, which every golfer experiences at least once, right? At least, that's the belief I used to have.

I have since had it clarified to me that not everyone who plays the game of golf actually does throw golf clubs in anger. Who knew?

I blame my propensity toward such action on my Scottish heritage. I have found myself crossing fairways and roads to retrieve clubs. One day I even found myself up a tree going after a misplaced seven iron—and the friends who accompanied me that day mention that climbing adventure at least once every time I see them.

More recent meltdowns have seen me destroying a very expensive pair of sunglasses after mildly tugging a ball out of bounds, and nearly killing myself after swinging a club at the trunk of a tree, only to discover that the laws of physics were not in my favor. The head of the club rather quickly orbited the trunk of the tree before breaking away from the shaft that once held it and slingshotting itself directly at my head.

Only a near miss allowed my continued survival. This would have provided good fodder for George Carlin.

My past contains many stories like these, of which I am not proud. In hindsight, I am actually quite appalled that I could ever have behaved in such a way. These stories, however, all pale in comparison to what I will now share with you.

The following is a story I sent to *Golf Digest* and Callaway Golf. Unfortunately, it was sad and true in every detail.

Dear Golf Digest:

"It seemed like a beautiful morning for golf. I and two of my friends headed out for the $15 early bird special (because we are all broke!) at one of our favorite local golf courses. The weather was brisk but beautiful and all signs seemed to point to a great round.

I was playing well, holing out a 20-footer to save par on the third hole and chipping in to save par on the fourth after giving away a shot to thrash my ball out of 8-inch rough following a straight drive of 300 yards that came up just short of the 329-yard hole.

The fifth hole was a routine par and left me at even par going to the sixth, a 531-yard par 5. This is where "the incident" occurred.

I hit what I thought was a good drive until I saw the water on the left about 270 yards out and decided I should play a provisional ball. This time I deliberately faded the ball away from the water hazard and drove out to play what would now be my fourth shot. Well, the ball was nowhere to be seen and I was learning a new lesson in patience.

The fairway slopes toward the water, which must have somehow tractor-beamed the ball into its murky depths. I then dropped what was shot number five behind the hazard and knew I needed to sink the 260-yard 3-wood to keep the par streak alive.

I set up to deliver the ball a mighty blow, expecting that the hours of hard work I had put in on the range would pay off. They didn't. The ball went 25 feet back into the lake.

Normally a temperate person, I was surprised to feel the heat rising inside me and smoke beginning to pour out of my ears. I consciously thought about throwing some kind of fit and decided I had every right to vent, so I struck my club three times against the earth as though it were to blame for my misfortune. This, however, did not provide the needed stress relief so I decided one more childish act was necessary.

I took aim at the middle of the fairway and threw my club as far as I could.

Unfortunately, because I had been squeezing it so hard, the club stuck to my glove and instead of traveling toward the fairway, took a left turn and headed—in slow motion, mind you—directly into the middle of the lake.

I watched in horror as my Callaway Warbird 3-wood that had been a reward for spending a ludicrous amount of money during a failed foray into a network marketing company--thereby having an actual value to me of several thousand dollars--disappeared into the dark pond. But wait! There was still hope!

The grip was peeking about one inch out of the top of the water. Perhaps the pond was only 45 inches deep and I could wade out and get my club! My friends laughed hysterically as I removed all of my lower clothing and wandered out into the icy water.

This water was deep and cold—and disgusting. In Arizona, to preserve water, many golf courses are watered with reclaimed sewer water that looks bad and smells even worse. Realizing that my hopes of wading were now dashed, I removed my remaining articles of clothing and threw them to shore.

By the time I was ten feet out into the lake, the water was over my head and I was forced to swim out and retrieve my club. I then swam back to shore and tried to make a quick and discreet escape from the foul liquid—as I was now buck naked—and needed to be sure that no one in the many houses lining the fairway was getting any unwanted entertainment over breakfast!

Mission accomplished! I dried off as best I could and got dressed, fearing my return home to a pregnant wife who was struggling with *good* smells, never mind the aroma that now clung to me. I was happy, though.

I had managed to save this great golf club and worse things could have happened than taking a ten on this hole. So, in keeping with remaining honorable to the rules of golf, I dropped another ball in the same spot as the first and decided to go at it one more time.

I forgot two very important things:. My hands were wet. The club was also wet. Sorry, three things: The shaft of the club had also filled with water as I swam to shore after retrieving it, making it much heavier than I could have been prepared for. I took one easy practice swing and gasped as the club slipped through my fingers and flew right back into the lake! This time it sank quickly below the surface and disappeared.

I know that I shouldn't have lost my temper, but was my sin so bad as to warrant this severe a punishment?

I miss my golf club tremendously, and I can't get a new one because Callaway no longer makes them. The experience hasn't been entirely bad, I guess. My friends thank me almost every day for giving them the best golf story they have ever seen or heard, and they are more than happy to testify to the truthfulness of every detail!"

Callaway sent me a little consolation package for that story. It contained a few golf gloves, a golf towel, and some golf balls. That was nice of them.

Several years passed, with endless practice sessions and rounds of golf played in the quest to impress.

I had a few more unpleasantries on the golf course but, for the most part, I steadily improved and managed to mostly beat the people I played with. (The exception was the people I wanted to beat most—my wife's brothers!)

As I worked my way to the point where I was a card-carrying 1-handicap, I never imagined the possibility of a day when I wouldn't look forward to being on the golf course. (As I grow older, I find it interesting how many things show up in my life that I previously never imagined possible.)

Then one gray night it happened—just as Jackie Paper had come no more to see Puff, the Magic Dragon—the love of golf left me.

I was asked by a friend if I would enjoy heading out for a free round later in that week and my response would have been shocking to nearly all who knew me: "NO," I said.

Something was drastically changing within me. "Free" and "Golf" combined in the same request should NEVER be greeted with a negative! Nevertheless, they had been, and with that began a new phase in my life. A phase where the perpetual pursuit of becoming a better golfer no longer drove my thoughts and occupied my time.

Fittingly, a period of grieving followed but, unlike the process learned during my brief study of psychology in college, this grieving process didn't flow through a series of phases and become less of a presence in my life.

Rather, there seemed to be a constant void that could not, would not, be filled. I found myself wandering through life "missing" the friend that golf had been to me throughout the years, even though it had been a fickle friend at best.

After a year-long effort at introspection and discovery of what was going on with me, I realized that it was time for me to find out why I had said "NO" to the invitation to free golf those many months previous. And what I found was eye-opening.

If you have ever witnessed a relationship where the people involved were not working with each other, then you will recognize what my relationship with golf had become.

It was as though golf was an abusive alcoholic and I was so lacking in self-esteem that I couldn't summon the courage to leave.

Every time I stepped on the course, I re-entered the world of self-destructive behavior that was certainly visible to those around me but not to myself.

I experienced little or no happiness when I played and often found myself pledging by the 14th hole that "this would be the last round of golf I would ever play!"

I am certain that this feeling resonates with many of my golfing friends and may resonate with you as you read. My certainty in stating this comes from the fact that I have heard many of those I have played golf with over the years proclaim — with a tremendous amount of conviction as they huffed and puffed their way off the 18th green — that they would not be back.

A very few of them have honored those pledges but many have experienced gaps in play similar to the one I was heading into.

When speaking with a friend of mine, with whom I had routinely golfed with when things were "going well," I mentioned that I would not be playing for a while and possibly not ever again. His response cut deep into my heart when he said, "Good. After our last round, I decided I probably wouldn't play with you again, anyway." Nice.

Now please understand, I am typically a rather fun person who enjoys people and laughing and being out doing things. The problem was that golf had become ridiculously important to me.

My identity was almost entirely wrapped up in how well I played. People had revered me as a good golfer—at least that's how I saw it—and routinely told stories about how far and well I could hit the ball.

I had become accustomed to being viewed with honor and respect when it came to golf! Sure, most other areas of my life left a lot to be desired. But golf! Now, that was something I could be proud of.

"IF YOU CAN'T EXPLAIN IT TO A SIX
YEAR OLD, YOU DON'T UNDERSTAND
IT YOURSELF."

ALBERT EINSTEIN

Chapter 5

Separation Anxiety

And so the lonely existence as a professed ex-golfer began.

The divorce was hard.

Sure, I pretended that I was doing well, but I was shutting out my partner of 30 years because we couldn't get along.

How well could I really be doing? I was certain that we just weren't supposed to be together anymore. We probably never should have been together in the first place.

The relationship had always been a little rocky but at least we had been able to hide it from others. In recent months, however, it had gotten so bad that my friends and family could see it and they didn't know how to help.

Inevitably, people I hadn't seen in a while would ask me about golf and I would get that uncomfortable tightness and sick feeling in my stomach.

Some of my friends were choosing sides and you can guess which side they chose. Pretty much everyone knew our break up was my fault but no one had the courage to tell me.

The hardest thing to deal with was when they would start to reminisce about "the old days" when things were good (at least on the surface) and we would all be out as couples having fun together.

Well, that was over now and my resolve was growing everyday that I would never go back. The relationship was unhealthy and it had to end!

We're still talking about golf, right?

Well, a couple of months passed and it didn't seem to be getting any easier for me.

It also happened that around this time, my good friend and mentor, Steve Chandler (look him up on line and read his books—you will be immeasurably grateful that you did!), created a school for those in the coaching profession—life, business, and personal development coaching—to more effectively get their powerful skills and message out to those who could be served by it.

One of the members of this Coaching School was a man by the name of Steve Tefsky. Steve, in a previous life, was a PGA Professional and taught golf as his vocation. Our experience with golf served to help us bond very quickly and we formed a friendship.

One of the methodologies employed by the coaching school to help us become better coaches was to partner up with "Peer Coaches" (someone else in the program with whom we would have regular coaching sessions over a period of time) and Steve and I agreed that for the period of one month, we would serve as peer coaches to each other.

For a month, we would meet together and coach each other in finding out what exactly we wanted and then finding which action steps we could take to create or produce what we wanted in our lives.

Steve decided that since we only lived a few miles from each other and both had a history with golf, we should hold our coaching sessions on the practice green and range of a local golf facility. It was only for a little putting, he assured me. It wasn't like golf and I were getting back together. Little did I know that making that choice would literally and powerfully change my life forever.

When we met on the practice green that spring morning, we decided that I would go first. I shared with him where I had gotten in my relationship with golf and explained that golf was no longer a priority in my life.

I continued by telling him that at one time I used to be fairly decent at the game in general, but at no time in my life was I ever able to putt very well.

My ophthalmologist had once told me that my vision was so impaired that reading greens would be like looking in a funhouse mirror for me and I would likely never become a great putter because of that condition.

Steve didn't buy into my excuse-making and had me put a few balls down as we talked.

He watched me take a few putts and observed that my putting was very consistent with what I had described. I missed left. I missed right. I missed short. I missed long. I pushed, I pulled, I yanked, I blocked. I did everything wrong that one could possibly do wrong when putting. In my mind I had proved the point that I just couldn't putt.

I WAS A BAD PUTTER. PERIOD.

What happened over the course of the next 20 minutes was nothing short of a miracle for me.

Steve had me change the position of the ball in my stance and talked to me about alignment. He pointed out that because of how I had been misaligning the putts, I had to guide and manipulate the putter and couldn't put a smooth repeatable stroke on the ball.

He asked me to make sure to make good contact with the ball and get it rolling smoothly. These were fairly simple changes, wouldn't you say?

Well, there is enormous beauty and reward in simplicity!

I did what he told me to do.

I moved the ball back in my stance and started focusing on how to strike the ball to get it rolling toward the hole from its new position. I was amazed at the change this one simple move created in the direction the ball rolled.

Strangely enough, now that I was aimed at the hole, that's where the ball seemed to go. What a novel idea!

We started with a little drill placing three balls three feet from the cup. In a typical round of golf, if I had five putts about three feet in length, I would miss four of them. I'm not kidding.

If you think you are a bad putter, be comforted in knowing that I was worse.

In my one attempt at passing a playing ability test necessary to become eligible to be a PGA Golf Instructor, I led the field in greens in regulation, but had 15 more putts than anyone else and missed the number by two shots!

So you can understand my astonishment as I made my first three putts in the drill.

I continued to be amazed as ball after ball dropped into the cup. We then proceeded to progress through this drill by moving a foot farther from the hole after each three putts until we were 10 feet away.

I spent the last 10 minutes of this putting lesson taking 50 putts from 10 feet. Steve kept track of makes and misses and when the last putt was struck and rolled purely down the line and dropped into the cup, he revealed the final tally: 38 makes in 50 attempts! I hadn't made more than five 10-foot putts in the entire last year of golfing!

Yes, every putt was from the same spot. Yes, it was just on a practice green. BUT I WAS STILL THE ONE SWINGING THE PUTTER and 38 out of 50 is something that I would not have believed possible just 20 minutes earlier!

How could such a remarkable change in results occur from such simple instruction in such a short period of time? That, I couldn't answer, but I did know that something awakened inside me that had at least re-lit the pilot light of love for golf.

It was time to have another crack at the relationship that I had selfishly abandoned, and this time it WOULD be different.

"SOMETIMES THE DREAMS THAT COME TRUE ARE THE DREAMS YOU NEVER EVEN KNEW YOU HAD."

ALICE SEBOLD

Chapter 6

The Epiphany

I had an epiphany.

Although not always the most authoritative source, I love this definition of epiphany taken directly from Wikipedia:

> "An **epiphany** (from the ancient Greek *epiphaneia*, manifestation, striking appearance") is an experience of sudden and striking realization. Generally, the term is used to describe breakthrough scientific, religious, or philosophical discoveries, but it can apply to any situation in which an enlightening realization allows a problem or situation to be understood from a **new and deeper perspective**.

> Psychologists and other scholars, particularly those attempting to study the process of innovation, study Epiphanies. Epiphanies are relatively rare occurrences and generally follow a process of significant thought about a problem. Often they are triggered by a new and key piece of information, but importantly, a depth of prior knowledge is required to allow the leap of understanding.

> The word epiphany originally referred to insight through the divine. Today, this concept is used much more often and without such connotations, but a popular implication remains that the epiphany is

supernatural, as the discovery seems to come suddenly from the outside."

I can think of no other way to define what occurred for me. I had been mired for months and even years in a dysfunctional relationship with a game that I reasonably should have had nothing but kind thoughts for.

It was as though the heavens opened and a voice spoke to me and said:

"Andrew. The relationship you have with golf is wrong and always has been wrong. The ONLY thing that matters is CONTACT. LOVE THAT, and everything else will fall into place."

This divine communication instantaneously cleared my mind of all the negativity and doubt that I had been carrying.

Suddenly, the old, dysfunctional relationship I had with golf was replaced with a new, vibrant relationship filled with love and gratitude!

I now saw the last 30 years from an entirely different perspective. Golf had never been bad to me; I had not been good to it.

When I began trying to relate this epiphany to those around me, I found it necessary to consider writing it down, and I did so with an enthusiasm I could not contain.

The driving range became like a little piece of heaven to me. I couldn't stay away. As I hit balls, excitement welled up inside me and people began to come up to me unsolicited and ask about what I was doing.

I have often observed that the number of people on a driving range who are frustrated is equal to the number of people on that driving range.

My new state changed that statistic. Now, there would be at least one person who loved what he was doing on the range and was frustration-free.

In all the years of golf I had played and practiced, I had never experienced anything like what I was currently experiencing.

In my passion and excitement, I became overjoyed at the prospect of sharing this with others! It was so clear and it was so simple. How could I never have thought of this before? At the very heart of The Epiphany was this truth:

The only thing that matters is contact.

Let me say that again more emphatically: THE ONLY THING THAT MATTERS IS CONTACT! Love that, and everything else will fall into place.

I had heard this or something like it before, but now I felt it to my core. It became part of who I was literally, in an instant, at least as much as it could at the time.

Nothing technical mattered anymore. Nothing emotional mattered. I didn't care where the ball went. I didn't care what my swing looked like. I sought out great contact between the center of the clubface and the golf ball and I loved it.

How and where the face of the golf club contacts the ball determines everything about where that golf ball will fly.

I know this seems simple. Because it is. And when you understand it to the depth of your core it will be enormously powerful in its simplicity. Please, stay with me. There is SO much more to it.

Although this is a simple concept and most golfers have at least heard it already, the experience of changing the way you understand this fact will change the way you exist as a golfer.

The "WHY" behind nearly every major flaw that occurs in golf is answered by this one simple concept! **THE ONLY THING THAT MATTERS IS CONTACT!**

The next question to ask is: "What is the WHY underneath the WHY?"

Now that we have established that making good contact is the key to the game of golf we must look at the things we've been taught to believe cause us to *not* make good contact.

Here is a short list that is in no way comprehensive.

1. Raising your head
2. Angle of approach too steep
3. Pulling the club across the ball (coming over the top)
4. Bad swing arc
5. Deceleration in the downswing (trying to guide the ball)
6. Hitting it thin-blading the ball
7. Lurching at the ball
8. Etc...

This list could easily have gone beyond 20, 30, or even 100 in number. A quick review of the last thousand golf publications would reveal that each has a list of "Tips" to address each one of these errors.

Tips are fun for the moment and may even seem to correct a problem. The issue with "tips" is that they are band-aids. They momentarily cover up a symptom without addressing the real problem. I will address "Tips" in more detail later!

Now, let's take a moment and try to get closer to identifying the actual root cause of all of these challenges.

What occurred to me first and may also have occurred to you is that all of this list can be created by TENSION. The golfer is trying too hard, forcing things. That creates tension.

True enough, but it's not enough for you to just tell yourself to quit trying so hard. You've got to understand *why* you are trying so hard.

So, if tension is not the real problem, what is? What is the underlying source of tension?

It is the underlying Why (WHY IS THERE TENSION?!) that must be answered. And the answer to that may be different for every person.

This is where the miraculous discovery occurred for me and it goes all the way back to that summer day long ago when my father eagled the 16th hole and unwittingly destroyed my confidence.

It was so deeply imbedded in my existence and so ever-present with me that I couldn't possibly have noticed it. You will most likely deny that it exists within you, as well. Welcome to the club that is humanity!

There is tension because I make every shot a determination of my value as a human being!

This is the part where everyone I share this idea with says, "I don't do that."

Let's look at that possibility.

Have you ever been embarrassed? What is embarrassment?

Once again, I like Wikipedia's definition:

"**Embarrassment** is an emotional state of intense discomfort with oneself, experienced upon having a socially unacceptable act or condition witnessed by or revealed to others. Usually some amount of loss of honor or dignity is involved, but how much and the type depends on the embarrassing situation."

Golf is a game in which we thrust ourselves into a position to repeatedly experience the very definition of embarrassment! There really is nothing else like it.

One could argue that dancing, public speaking, or any number of activities could do the same and I would agree. That is why we generally, and with great effort, avoid most of those activities.

But golf is different. Socially, it's supposed to be fun. It's not something that the masses avoid. Instead, it is a game where we PRETEND that we don't care how well we do, but how we play is an absolute giveaway that we DO care. I know, I've played with many of you and many of you have played with me.

We are lying to ourselves by saying that we don't care how well we play. The proof of this self-deception is laid out clearly before the world every time we swing the club.

When we say we don't care, we are lying to ourselves; until we're not.

The brilliant psychotherapist Nathaniel Branden, in his book *The Six Pillars of Self-Esteem*, explains that the reason adults don't learn things is because they are unwilling to expose their egos to the blow that learning requires.

Getting to the real answer of why there is tension will require something of a blow to the ego, but the blow is far less painful than we imagine it to be and enormously liberating once received!

I have so much enjoyment now when I'm on the range or playing golf, I feel like I'm channeling the ghost of Barry White. The other day I said "Oh, Yeah" under my breath so many times that the guy beside me asked if he could have some of what I was having!

The beautiful thing about this request is that, YES, he can have what I am having. And he can have it much more easily than he could ever imagine.

The rest of this book is dedicated to explaining how.

"YOU NEED THE SIMPLEST VERSION OF THE IDEA IN ORDER FOR IT TO GROW NATURALLY IN THE SUBJECT'S MIND."

EAMES [INCEPTION]

Chapter 7

The Concept

Let me begin this chapter by saying that it is the most important chapter of the book.

It is the centerpiece; the central message. Everything that came before did so with the purpose of introducing the message of this chapter. Everything that comes after does so to reinforce the message of this chapter.

I want you to get this. I want you to feel it in a way that's as meaningful to you as it has been for me. This is the game changer. And it can be much more than just a game changer.

Let me repeat that: **THIS IS THE MOST IMPORTANT CHAPTER IN THIS BOOK.**

If you get nothing else out of this book, I at least hope that from now on when you hear the term "The Concept", it brings your mind to what I am about to share with you. I will do my best to come at it and support it from every angle so that it sticks.

The Concept is what came to my mind with The Epiphany and it is this:

The only thing that matters in golf is contact. Love that and everything else will fall into place.

If I stopped there and you got the full meaning of that statement, it would be enough. There would be no need to go on. But even as the earthly author of this statement, I haven't yet grasped the FULL meaning of The Concept and I certainly will not deny myself the opportunity to explore it as completely as possible. So, go on I will.

If you happen to be a non-golfer (how that could be, I struggle to understand!) it is necessary to explain to you that there is a frequency created by pure contact between clubface and golf ball that gives feedback to your soul in the same way a glorious chord played by a world class orchestra does.

You will KNOW when it happens. It will move you.

THAT is the thing that keeps people coming back. There is nothing like it! It resonates throughout your body and mind. It is magnificent. It is spiritual! I love it.

When I coach a client, I explain that the beginning golfer doesn't know what it feels like to create pure contact. But as soon as they feel it, they will seek to do it again and again.

That beginning golfer may soon get to the point where they experience pure contact on one out of every ten or twenty shots.

Coaching and practice (necessarily in that order) will help them increase the frequency of it until they progress to the level of a good amateur who may create pure contact five or six times out of ten.

The ultimate accomplishment is to reach the level of a pro who may manage the feat eight or nine times out of ten.

Good contact cannot be forced. It cannot be manipulated. It cannot be made to happen. When circumstances are right, it WILL happen.

The right circumstances include peace and clarity of mind. They include absolute freedom from tension. The beauty is that you CAN be in control of those circumstances; just not in the way you may think.

Let's now visit the circumstances we want to create to greatly enhance the probability of creating good contact and experience the joy that goes along with it.

To start, let's return to the quote on the title page of this book.

"90 percent of all golfers never see the club hit the ball."

To join the roughly 10 percent who do see the club hit the ball and ultimately, to have that group grow substantially larger, we have to WANT to see the club make contact with the ball.

Most people say that they do want to see the club hit the ball and I respond by saying that their actions prove otherwise. At least they prove there is something they want more that's occurring at the same moment.

Byron Kathleen Mitchell, better known as Byron Katie, an American speaker and author who teaches a method of self-inquiry known as "The Work," shares a thought that I have come to value enormously. She says:

"If I had a prayer, it would be this: 'God spare me from the desire for love, approval, and appreciation. Amen."

This quote embodies the deepest reason we don't see the club hit the ball.

We want to feel good about ourselves, to feel valued as humans, to have others appreciate how good we are.

In our impatience to fill this need as we golf, we do many things. We try to manipulate the club into the "right" position. We try to swing the club as fast as Bubba Watson. We look up prematurely to validate that we have hit a good shot and have proven that we are as good as we hoped we were and, in doing so, blade the ball and hit it into a water hazard! Any of that sound familiar?

So how do we change this?

The things required to change this are contrary to human nature. They are contrary to human nature because it actually is human nature to do all those things.

It will take effort in the form of coachability, patience, and relaxation.

It will take effort to see things differently than we have ever seen them.

It will take effort for us to admit things about ourselves that are uncomfortable to admit. It will require effort for us to give ourselves permission to fail.

It will require effort UNTIL we discover that it doesn't require effort.

Nearly everything we typically do to try to hit good golf shots is absolutely contrary to The Concept.

Trying to force the club to travel along a certain path by manipulating it will only serve to create tension and will sabotage your desired result.

Trying to hit the ball HARD will only serve to create tension.

Worrying about whether you are swinging correctly will only serve to create doubt and tension.

Fear of a bad result will create tension.

What we need to do to create this change is Let Go. Let go of the belief that we have to hit good shots. We don't.

We must let go of the expectation of perfection coupled with the fear that we cannot live up to that expectation. We need to let go and then we need to love.

The first thing to do is to eliminate, or at least greatly minimize, the opportunity for self-judgment. This occurs naturally by having the ball and contact with it as the only things to focus on.

When I first experienced The Concept for myself following The Epiphany, I didn't pick targets when I hit balls at the range. For the first couple of months following The Epiphany, when I went to the range I had what I called "No Target Practice." That was one of the methodologies I used to be certain that I wasn't emotionally attached to the outcome of the shot.

There can be no judgment when there is no standard by which to judge.

I learned to focus only on contact and I learned to love doing only that.

The more focus and love you bring to the action of placing the clubface on the ball, the less room there is for any other thoughts to creep in and steal your joy (and destroy your results!)

This is not, however, intended to remove standards from our lives, rather to create an opportunity for us to have an awareness of how much our attachment to those standards wreaks havoc on us.

There is only contact followed by observation.

You may learn from that observation and apply minor changes to your contact, but please do not judge yourself. You are neither a bad person nor a good person based on how you hit a golf ball.

In the 1963 movie musical *West Side Story* (this is an interesting example because it is also the first musical that I played a lead role in—more about that later), Tony saw Maria across a crowded dance floor and was smitten with love!

This was, to me, one of the greatest uses of visual effects in movie history as everything in the room became blurry to Tony except for Maria standing on the other side of the room.

It was an exceptional demonstration of tunnel vision and single-minded focus. Everything else at that moment became completely meaningless. Tony saw only Maria even though the room was filled with teenagers shouting and moving.

This is very similar to the experience that I began to have on the golf range immediately after The Concept came to me. I would stand there and look down at that ball and make a connection with it having no thought or interest or even awareness of anything going on around me. Everything else became blurry to me and completely unnoticeable in my vision. That focus remained until I struck the ball with the golf club.

My entire life I have been plagued with an inability to focus. I was always the kid whose desk was right next to the teacher's in my early years in school. I once had my desk moved to the lobby of the school on a trial basis to see if that would cure my problem of keeping my classmates from doing their work.

Isolation seemed to be the Canadian behavior modification method of choice when I was young. It never worked on me.

In the years following grade school, my lack of focus caused me huge amounts of grief and challenge and had become such an accepted part of my life that what I was now experiencing post-Epiphany should have been shocking to me.

Somehow, it wasn't shocking.

Experiencing this kind of focus felt so good and was so much fun that I didn't even think about being shocked in the midst of my enjoyment.

Moe Norman, a fellow Canadian and a person generally considered to be the greatest ball striker in the history of golf, seemed to have a condition that was nearly opposite to mine that allowed him to focus perfectly on hitting golf balls.

In fact, he was such a remarkable ball striker that an entire movement in golf was patterned after him called Natural Golf.

During the Natural Golf craze, I saw people on driving ranges all around the world imitating the positions that Moe would put the club in when he swung it.

It was strange to look at because, to me, it seemed anything but natural. But if Moe could create the results he created with that swing, it must be the best way to swing! Right?

There was only one major problem with this. It wasn't Moe Norman's swing or technique that made him a great striker of the golf ball; it was his mind.

You see, Mr. Norman was obsessed with ball striking. He simply did not mishit shots. There was a good reason.

Friends and people who knew him will tell you that he was different from nearly everyone else. He was very antisocial and had a hard time relating to others. He may have had a form of high-functioning autism. Whatever it was, it helped him think about only one thing when he played golf.

He may have been the ultimate expression of the application of The Concept. He ALWAYS saw the club hit the ball. Nothing could distract him from it. He simply did not care about anything outside of contact and he loved what he did.

The rest of us, on the other hand, have an amazing tendency to look up toward our target before we ever hit the ball with the club.

My dad is a carpenter.

I grew up watching him build things. He always seemed to have a hammer in his hand or at least very near by. Those memories brought an analogy to my mind that really made a lot of sense to me and I shared it with him.

Imagine you have a hammer in your hand and you are getting ready to drive a nail into a piece of wood. You place the nail on the spot where you want it to go and then you prepare to hit the head of the nail with the hammer.

You waggle the hammer several times to make sure that you feel just right about how you're going to swing it. You then pull your arm away from the nail to take a couple of practice swings with the hammer, being sure to emulate what you believe is a perfect hammer swing.

You then hover the hammerhead over top of the nail and start thinking. Oh no, here comes the nervous tension. You are now worrying if you're going to hit the nail the right way. "What if I hit it poorly? Will people laugh at me? I am horrible at hammering!"

You wind back with the hammer, manipulating your hand and making sure that you'll make the perfect swing along the proper arc while maintaining the wrist angle the pros have taught that you must have to successfully pound a nail.

As you start the downward descending blow with the hammer, you worry about how you're going to contact the nail and you think that maybe it won't go exactly where it's supposed to go, so just before you strike the hammerhead on the head of the nail, you lean down and look underneath the board to make sure that you see that the nail has gone through the board exactly as you wanted it to and you miss the nail entirely! Shoot!

I know this sounds incredibly ridiculous, but isn't this exactly what we do every time we set up to a golf ball and look up during the swing to see where the ball is going? Heaven forbid we should stay focused on the ball and give ourselves the best chance to hit it!

The psychology of golf is an interesting thing. We can swing a hammer just perfectly when there is no nail to hit. And even Charles Barkley can make a good-looking swing when he doesn't have a golf ball on the ground in front of him! (By the way, if you have never seen video of him trying to hit a golf ball, then you've made good choices.)

I don't think it's necessary to ask the question anymore why the presence of the golf ball changes everything for Sir Charles and likely for most of us. I think we have established why that is. Our goal now is to progress down the road of changing the relationship we have with the golf ball.

The key to this is love. Learn to love contact to the exclusion of all other emotion or thought. Have that love be completely unconditional.

What conditions are we putting on loving the creation of contact? Removal of these conditions frees us from tension and allows purity to flow in.

The PUREST CONTACT occurs in the place where no conditions exist to prevent it!

In my quest to find a publication that in any way described what I felt The Concept teaches, I searched through books, the Internet, and magazines. Finally, I found something in the May 2012 issue of *GOLF Magazine*.

Touring professional Retief Goosen gives a Tour Tip titled "How to Catch Every Drive Square." The subtitle is the little piece of gold that I was searching for: "MAKE THE BALL YOUR TARGET, NOT THE FAIRWAY"

In the tip, he identifies the problem of having different balance and rhythm on different shots and that will cause you to catch the ball anywhere but in the center of the clubface.

The solution he offers to alleviate this problem in the moment is to "PICK OUT A DIMPLE ON THE BACK OF THE BALL. YOUR ONLY GOAL WHEN YOU START YOUR SWING IS TO DRIVE THE CENTER OF YOUR CLUBFACE INTO THAT DIMPLE. Narrowing your focus like this automatically centers your swing—you'll be less likely to sway, lift or dip and, as a result, you'll have a better chance of nailing your contact point."

BRAVO, BRAVO, Retief!!

He goes on to say that he finds this technique especially effective when the pressure starts to mount. Of course!

As soon as meaning is added to something, hope and fear come with it, bringing tension that sabotages the desired result. Focusing on result will do that, but only 100% of the time.

In going back to take a closer look at Retief's tip, he absolutely hits the nail on the head (as we have already discussed!) in recommending that we narrow our focus to making contact between the center of the clubface and a dimple on the ball.

He also gets very close to identifying the problem but doesn't really address it, probably because it doesn't occur to him. The level at which he thinks about golf is much different than the average golfer.

As we become more adept at seeking the WHY beneath the WHY, we will quickly be able to identify that being off balance and having poor rhythm are not the real problem, only symptoms of the real problem. The real problem isn't even the tension that is creating the lack of good balance or rhythm.

The REAL problem is the SOURCE of the tension, which in turn creates poor rhythm and balance. And that source of tension is that our minds and energy are focused on hitting a good shot to spare ourselves the discomfort of the blow that will be administered to our self-esteem if we should happen to hit a bad one!

I suppose you are wondering if part of The Concept is to continually return to the idea that self-esteem is inseparably connected to how well I play and I'm only playing poorly because of my desire for the love and approval of others.

The answer is no. Once you have become aware of the root cause of the tension you are experiencing with golf, you don't need to think about it anymore. You will be free to move on. It will liberate you and give you the freedom to embrace The Concept.

You may ask yourself, "How will I know if I have fully understood The Concept?"

The answer is this: You will know that The Concept has permeated you and embedded itself in your very soul as a golfer when you no longer have a desire during a round of golf to see or experience anything other than pure contact between the center of the clubface and the golf ball.

You will no longer look up prior to creating contact because you won't want to!

This is golfing enlightenment.

"LIFE IS REALLY SIMPLE,
BUT WE INSIST ON MAKING
IT COMPLICATED."

CONFUCIUS

CHANGE YOUR GAME, CHANGE YOUR LIFE - 67

Chapter 8

Barriers to Application

It's here where I almost have to shout a simple "if/then" question to myself.

"IF" the Concept works (and I know that it does!), "THEN" WHY ON EARTH do I not apply it?

The answer to that can be both simple and complex.

Let's take a deep breath and choose simplicity. The simple approach is to identify these barriers and question them without trying to figure out why they are there and without denying that they exist.

What are the barriers to applying The Concept?

The barriers are identical to the barriers to good judgment.

If we were making decisions in a vacuum, absent of stress and fear of past failure, equally absent of worry and fear about desired future outcome, and most importantly, absent of concern about how we will be perceived by others around us, we would be equipped to make effective decisions.

There are a number of mental barriers that we have erected over a lifetime that create resistance or blockades for something as simple as The Concept to remain uppermost in our minds.

The list of barriers could be rather long, but to most effectively illustrate and then work to remove them, we will limit the barriers in this discussion to a manageable few.

Each one of these barriers deserves at the very least a longer discussion than we will go into here or even a book of its own (at least one WILL be getting its own book!) but for now, this short list will have to do.

The first is CLARITY.

We walk onto the golf course for a round of golf with a "pretend" idea that we know what we want. We want to have fun. Ha! I've seen the same person claiming to be motivated by "fun" throwing their clubs into a lake by the 6th hole! I've been that person on more than one occasion (as you now know)!

And I'm not saying that everyone is lying when they say they play for fun. Everyone isn't lying…just mostly everyone. Let's be honest. Fun is a politically correct cover-up for why we are really there.

Our minds are so muddled with different thoughts on the golf course that we couldn't possibly have clarity. We have 186 tips running through our minds from the last fifty golf publications we've read or DVDs and TV shows we've watched, and each tip is eager to step to the forefront every time we hit a bad shot!

That is just one more reason to be "anti-golf-tip!" Tips destroy clarity!

Let's take a moment and honestly measure our golf on a "Frustration Scale."

On a scale of 1-10, what is your frustration level with your golf game? A ten on this scale means you're frustrated with every aspect of your golf game and find no enjoyment playing whatsoever. Scoring a 0 would mean that you are completely content and euphoric to the point that you never experience any frustration and you love every aspect of your game unconditionally.

My guess is that your score will fall somewhere between these numbers, but I want to help you get as close to 0 as you can be. Scoring zero on this scale is a far greater accomplishment than having a zero on the handicap index!

Clarity doesn't often hang out with frustration.

We want to play well but we have no clear game plan to do it. Hitting and hoping is not clarity.

We want to bring what we learned on the range to the course.

The problem with that is what we do on the range doesn't transfer to the course because it only involves technical practice, not mental! At least, not until we learn the right things to do on the range.

Becoming clear in the simplicity of how we approach the game both on the range and on the course will dramatically raise our enjoyment and performance and diminish the list of barriers that keep us from implementing The Concept.

PHYSICAL TENSION

Sometimes we have real physical limitations to doing something that we think is necessary to achieve a certain outcome.

Let's say, for example, that I have a broken leg. That broken leg is a real physical limitation to playing soccer and when I step onto the field, I do not compete very well.

Of course I don't! I have a broken leg!

Most of us, also, do not have the flexibility of Rory McIlroy or Justin Rose and can't possibly move the club around our bodies the way they do. Why then do we have in our minds that we must turn the same distance they do to achieve golfing success? Why do we try?

We try because we are subconsciously programmed to compare ourselves and our golf swings to others. We try because we are inwardly unhappy with ourselves and believe we need to be more like someone else.

That seems ridiculous, doesn't it? Prove it wrong. Please. I would feel better about myself if it were.

That is why I love a recent commercial for the PGA Tour that features Arnold Palmer inviting all who play the game of golf to stop seeking perfection in how they swing the club and simply "Swing your swing" and find the joy in that. He concludes his invitation by saying, "I know I certainly did."

The King has certainly been THE example of "how to love what you do" and the results followed without placing too much emphasis on them.

The most common barrier to The Concept that I see on golf courses and driving ranges around the world is that nearly everyone takes the club back to a place that creates tension for them. They take the club back too far. In other words, they are FORCING themselves into a position of physical limitation.

The moment you have taken the club back to a point where there is unnecessary tension—that is, tension in muscles that are not part of swinging the club—you have added obstacles that you now need to overcome and compensate for as you bring the club down to create contact. Let the manipulation begin!

If you have a physical limitation, acknowledge it. Pretending that you can play through something does not increase your enjoyment of the game and will only lead to more frustration and unwanted tension, which in turn will likely lead to further physical limitation!

There are two ways to deal with a physical limitation. You can either shorten your swing or increase your flexibility. I recommend doing both!

I recently had an injury to my back and was very impatient with it.

While lying in yoga class one day, I let my mind identify where the resistance to relaxation was coming from in my body, to the point where that injury became invisible to my mind.

I know that requires a clearer explanation.

As I discovered where the tiny discomfort was, I realized that all the tension around it was just my mind's way of trying to protect myself from that tiny bit of pain.

In so doing, my mind had created a large area of tension that disrupted my enjoyment of basically everything in my life. It didn't have to be like that.

If I were sedated, for example, or in a very deep sleep, my body would no longer be receiving signals from my mind to protect itself from the slightest discomfort.

PAY AT-TENSION

It was at that moment in yoga class that I thought of this term. I didn't want to just "Pay attention" to the pain, I wanted to "Invest in discovering exactly where the source of pain was so that I could release all the unnecessary tension around it!"

Invest yourself in discovering where the tension lies in you.

It is also important to recognize that the tension is usually not where you think it is. That's your barrier to enjoyment.

It will take awareness to find it.

This is where the tension was in the moment. It was created out of a desire to protect. The desire was falsely placed because it didn't succeed in protecting me from pain but rather in creating a scenario where I was acutely aware of my pain. That acute awareness then destroyed my ability to enjoy anything I was doing.

PROTECTING OURSELVES

When you set up for a golf shot, what is it you may be protecting yourself from or against? It is a question very worth asking and an honest response will almost always reveal something.

Are you protecting yourself from hitting it left? Are you protecting yourself from hitting it right? Is there water that you are trying to avoid? Are you protecting against a hook or a slice?

Are you protecting yourself from some perceived pain that you think you might experience from a mild injury?

We sometimes believe if we relax ourselves and let ourselves go, that somehow we will feel this pain.

The truth of the matter is that the creation of all these protections creates tension and sabotages our results. We don't need these protections. We don't need any of them.

It is in finding FREEDOM from protecting ourselves that our love, focus, and relaxation can flow.

RIGHTNESS

We have most likely all heard the statement "Would you rather be right or would you rather be happy?"

The statement offers a powerful truth. You CANNOT BE RIGHT AND HAPPY. The two conditions cannot exist in the same space at the same time, much like love and fear.

What that statement does NOT mean, however, is that you must be WRONG to be happy. NO! This is where a shift in traditional thinking is required.

We have been taught that everything in this world is either right or wrong. Not true. Everything is not either right or wrong, it just is.

Even if you are a person who believes in Absolute Truth in some areas, you must be open to the fact that not everything can be determined as being either right or wrong.

How does having an attitude of needing to be right impact our golf? It creates enormous tension, that's how.

We say we want peace and then we cling to rightness. There is no peace in being right. The absence of peace results in the absence of a quiet mind.

Rightness: having a subconscious, preconceived notion of what you are "supposed to do" that is inflexible in adapting to other possibilities.

My son Jacob, who is very attached to the notion that everything needs to be done "the RIGHT WAY," was working on some physical training during the writing of this book.

One day he was in my office doing pushups and was having a terrible time. The placement of his hands was making pushups nearly impossible for him! They were way out to the sides and up about the level of the top of his head.

I tried to get him to put them a little closer to his shoulders, but he was extremely resistant. He had an idea in his head of "the right way" to do pushups and was unwilling to do them "the wrong way!"

First, I must say that I greatly admire his built-in desire to do the right thing. It will stand him in good stead in so many areas of his life and his future employers will love him for it!

The problem, as evidenced in Jacob's pushup example, occurs when what we think is right, isn't.

You may be completely unaware of this, but you most likely have a full instruction manual in your subconscious mind of what you think are the right things to do when it comes to golf.

Your attachment to that "rightness" is creating tension in you and making learning, change, and adaptation very difficult.

You don't even know it's happening!

Your freedom to relax and create pure contact is completely limited by subconscious beliefs that the club "Needs" to be in a certain position for your swing to be "RIGHT."

There is no "RIGHT WAY!" Remember what Arnold said: There is a way that works for you to create pure contact through love and relaxation and then there are other ways that don't.

Letting go of "being right" is one of the greatest things you can do for your golf game! Your enjoyment level will skyrocket! Your energy level will increase! Your ability to relax will multiply! And your results, even though you're not focused on them, will improve dramatically!

Inside of each one of us there is, to some degree, a child who is still asking the question, "Am I doing this right?" as though there really were a "RIGHT" way to be doing things. Let's be aware of that child and let him or her know that it's more than ok to just LOVE what you are doing and DO IT.

TRYING TOO HARD

Let's proceed with the "I love this in others" test.

A very common issue that amateur and often professional golfers have is that they TRY SO HARD.

Trying hard is never effective and only serves to create tension.

Trying is born out of doubt and expectation. The foundation upon which "trying" rests is very unstable. Trying too hard is a dysfunctional mental approach, which can only produce poor results.

When I am walking up to my ball, I remind myself of this possible mental flaw by repeating this phrase: "You know what I really love in a person? I love when they are trying too hard."

We all know that person. The one who just tries too darn hard. They TRY to be funny. They TRY to be friendly. They TRY to be clever. You know them. You may have been them. I have.

You don't want to be that person. You especially don't want to be that person when you're playing golf. It doesn't work.

Yoda showed the greatness of his wisdom when he said, "Do, or do not. There is no try."

In the presence of love, all the trying disappears.

While on the range recently, I was hitting balls next to a friend of mine who is a professional golfer. His ball flight is immaculate and a thing of beauty to behold and I was admiring it with great attention when he said to me, "That is a great ball mark pattern right in the middle of your clubface." He was referring to the place on my club where the mark shows where I consistently strike the ball.

Through thirty years of golfing, lessons, and exhaustive amounts of practice, I had never had a wear pattern on my golf clubs that I could be proud of. Rather, the ball marks would always be up on the face or out toward the toe of the club.

Someone had tried too hard produced those contact points.

I was that someone. I tried too hard. I actually made it work for me. Until I snapped.

I was striking the ball toward the toe of the club even when I was a 1-handicap! I had practiced so hard and so much that I had overcome a tremendous flaw in how I struck the ball.

That kind of off-center contact was robbing me of distance, control, and above all, it was robbing me of the joy of feeling pure contact! I was robbing myself by trying too hard!

I was robbing myself of a far more enjoyable golfing life than I ever could have imagined and I didn't even know it.

There are many other barriers to applying The Concept that I'll save for a later time. The most important question for you is, "What are my barriers?" I invite you to be as honest as you possibly can. Discovering what your real barriers are will allow you to challenge and dismiss them!

What does every single one of these barriers we've just addressed have as a common trait?

They are all **THOUGHTS THAT DRAW US AWAY FROM WHAT REALLY MATTERS**.

We can call them whatever we want, but they are not unique in how they disrupt or in the type of barrier they create to the implementation of The Concept.

They ALL keep us from focusing on and loving the contact we create between club and ball, and thereby add tension where tension is not welcome.

"SIMPLICITY IS A GREAT VIRTUE BUT IT REQUIRES HARD WORK TO ACHIEVE IT AND EDUCATION TO APPRECIATE IT. AND TO MAKE MATTERS WORSE: COMPLEXITY SELLS BETTER."

ERNST F. SCHUMACHER

Chapter 9

This Is as Technical as I Will Get

In 50 years, the average handicap hasn't gone down. How can that be?

Equipment has improved by leaps and bounds. The ball has improved even more. Courses are in better condition and greens are much easier to putt on. The amount of teaching and training available has multiplied exponentially!

Why, then, has the average score of the weekend golfer remained the same? Why? Because the average mentality of that golfer hasn't changed!

We are still using the same method of learning a new tip until it doesn't work and then moving on to the next. We are still just as attached to outcome as we ever have been! Maybe even more so now that social media has made our lives so public!

Scores cannot improve until there is a shift in psychology.

The pros understand this. Nearly every professional golfer has a golf or sports psychologist they work with. I can hear it in nearly every press conference and interview. They use catch phrases like staying in the moment, taking one shot at a time, enjoying myself out there.

These are phrases that were present with guys like Jack Nicklaus and Arnold Palmer years ago because they were naturals at the mental game. They probably didn't understand entirely at that time that their greatest advantage was mental. Now, every golfer from the first to the thousandth ranked golfer says the same things.

I bring this up because this is the one teaching that hasn't trickled down to amateur golf. Amateur and weekend golfers are STILL stuck on technical instruction. They have the order wrong! They think they need to get technically sound and THEN add the mental training, when the opposite is true.

That being said, there *are* a couple of technical elements that we want to solidify, which will give us the best possibility of enjoying the game.

Grip.

Make sure you have a good one. There are two standards from which to choose. They are:

- The Overlap and
- The Interlock

I use an overlap grip because I believe it puts less stress on my hands and wrists than the interlock. It also helps me be more relaxed and anything that does that is good in my book. (Actually, in MY BOOK!)

I cannot, however, argue with the effectiveness of the interlock grip, as the two greatest golfers of all time use it.

You can research these grips online or in golf books and try them out. Go to your local pro and have him or her work with you on your grip. After nearly thirty years of golfing with an interlock grip, I switched to the overlap at the time of The Epiphany. I did this under the direction of Steve Tefsky and have never looked back. I love this grip!

Posture.

You can research this online or have a pro help you with this, as well.

Some keys of good golf posture are to make sure you have a nice, relaxed, athletic stance when addressing the ball. You are bent at the hips, knees flexed, feet roughly shoulder-width apart. Your back is straight, but not stiff. Your arms should be relaxed and hanging freely in front of you. No slouching.

There is an endless number of resources to help you achieve this. The relaxed part will be taken care of by applying The Concept.

You have now set yourself up to create enjoyable, pure contact with the golf ball. You have a good grip and good posture. Your mind is quiet and you are meditative in your stillness. You have no part of you that is trying to make the ball go somewhere.

The other elements that most people would assume are also technicalities that need to be addressed before you start hitting golf balls are:

Setup and Alignment

Setup relates to a whole host of conditions, including ball position. Alignment, obviously, has to do with what direction you are aimed. I don't want to get wrapped up in "the perfect setup" and "the correct" alignment. Doing so is not helpful and is unnecessary when using the "no-target" practice approach.

I don't want anything to take you away from the focus on making good contact and nothing else. When contact is made, you may observe how that contact influences the ultimate destination of the ball and THAT will help to determine ball position and alignment on subsequent shots.

My suggestion is simply to EXPERIMENT with your setup and alignment and to embrace the following golfing mantra that eliminates self-judgment:

Contact ➜ Observation ➜ Next!

The last thing I want to do is introduce anything that will make it more difficult for you to observe what you are creating, free of judgment. I absolutely do not want to "over-teach" and create confusion in your mind.

Through experimentation, you will quickly arrive at an understanding of how different ways of creating contact produce different results in terms of where the ball goes.

Remember that TENSION IS NOT YOUR FRIEND.

Tension will not improve your golf game. Thoughts that invite tension in are thoughts that should be invited out.

Most thoughts invite tension and therefore should be invited out or never allowed to enter in the first place. These thoughts can be removed by bringing love and focus to the action we are involved in, which is creating contact between the clubface and the golf ball.

If this seems to be getting very repetitive, that's because it is.

I have two analogies that I use to help bring absolute focus to the moment of contact.

The first involves a discussion of Swing Plane.

When I am coaching, I do not allow my clients to select a target on the range.

I don't want them to be concerned with alignment or anything else involved in where the ball goes. I will refer to the swing as a two-plane swing but not in the conventional sense. The plane I'm referring to is intended to turn "The Moment of Contact" into a two-dimensional event.

This is the plane I consider to be the most important in golf. You have most likely heard of keeping your swing "on plane" and quite a bit of technical talk about the plane that your club follows during a backswing and downswing. That plane, to me, is irrelevant for the purposes of what we are discussing in this book.

Imagine that you're addressing the golf ball in your setup position. Now visualize swinging the club and creating contact with the ball.

At the point where the clubface comes in contact with the ball, I want you to visualize a line that extends out infinitely behind you and infinitely out in front of you through that point. Look at the illustration to clearly understand what I am describing.

This plane intersects at the exact point that the club will contact the golf ball and represents that instant in time. It helps me to imagine a giant, razor thin pane of glass that is perfectly dividing two things for me.

In front of this plane, (or pane of glass) in the direction the golf ball will travel AFTER being struck, is THE FUTURE. Everything behind this plane is THE PAST.

My intention is to become so involved with what happens at the instant the club strikes the ball — or "THE PRESENT" — that nothing about the future or the past has any meaning to me. I do this for one major reason: to release tension.

You see, tension is the enemy to creating successful contact with the golf ball. I am not suggesting that the past doesn't matter or have an influence on what happens at contact.

What I AM suggesting is that you are creating tension in yourself by being emotionally or mentally attached to any things that are in the past such as:

- o Is the clubface open or closed?
- o Am I on plane?
- o Did I take the club too far outside?
- o Am I coming over the top?
- o …And every other swing thought that we have been exposed to after years of ingesting so much technical teaching and so many golf tips

With this visual of a pane of glass separating the past and future at the point of contact, our minds can be completely invested in that moment of contact.

The goal now is not just to see the clubface strike the ball purely, but also to do it in a way that it shatters that pane of glass! Feel the club whip through that pane of glass and relax as that shattered glass falls to the ground!

This analogy helped one client of mine do something that he had never done in nearly forty years of playing golf! He reached a 500-yard par 5 in two shots!

This idea of speed through relaxation was something new to him.

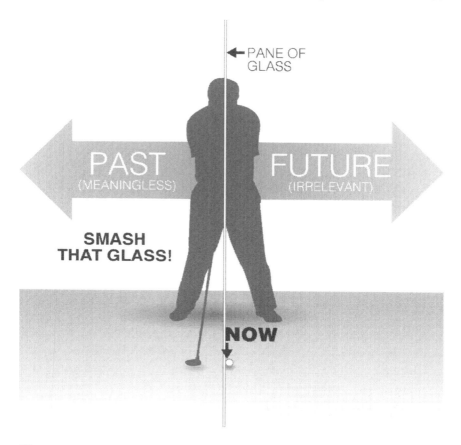

This is a simple graphic to illustrate the analogy of "The One Plane Swing: Smash the Glass!"

The top illustrates the idea of the pane of glass extending infinitely behind and in front of me. My eyes are focused on the back of the ball where the imaginary pane of glass intersects as illustrated in the fabulous lower drawing. All my focus, attention, and love is on creating contact at that point. That is where how I will smash the glass!

Faster. Not harder.

Speed is accomplished through increasing relaxation and decreasing tension.

As entertaining as it is when certain professional golfers go after shots in a violent way, it doesn't increase their likelihood of achieving a specific outcome.

Even if that desired outcome is having the ball travel a greater distance, it is more likely to do so if violence is removed from the swing and relaxation is brought to it. Relax through the swing. Love the contact.

There is no violence in love.

The second analogy or illustration that I use is a simple way to help you create different ball flights from the contact you make. When you select which dimply on the ball you wish to contact with the center of the clubface, your body and mind collaborate subconsciously to produce the action that will create that contact.

If the dimple is in the lower half of the inside of the ball, the path of the club will come from inside and will promote a right to left (for a right-handed golfer) ball flight, or a high draw. If the spot you choose is higher on the outside half of the ball, you will naturally bring the club from outside in and create a low fade. Please go out and try this.

This one approach to ball flight has possibly been the most popular thing strangers on the range have approached me and asked about after overhearing it.

In closing, the only technical approach I bring to golfing is to remember the things contained in the following paragraph:

Establish a good grip and love it. Find a solid, relaxed stance with good posture and love that. Now, in a relaxed, serene way, simply draw your focus in to the event that you love: The contact of clubface with golf ball.

This is a beautiful act that will not bring frustration or any other negative emotion when being enjoyed for what it is. Remove expectation and trying to force a specific result and the peaceful enjoyment of the activity will permeate your experience.

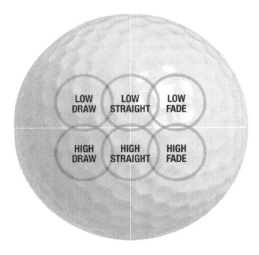

This is a very basic illustration of how to choose which dimple to focus on based on the ball flight you would like to produce. For example, if I wish to hit a high draw, then I find a dimple on the lower inside back of the golf ball and create contact with that spot. I do not worry about technical changes in my swing to produce the high draw ball flight. My mind body automatically adjust to create those changes when I seek to produce contact between the clubface and that dimple on the ball. It is literally that simple.

The higher on the ball I create contact, the lower the ball flight, and so on. This is a lot of fun to experiment with!

"I NEVER MADE ONE OF MY
DISCOVERIES THROUGH THE
PROCESS OF RATIONAL
THINKING"

ALBERT EINSTEIN

Chapter 10

Five Things That Can Be Better for Your Golf Game than Practicing Golf

You will get more benefit to your golf game by doing these five things than by going to the range and hitting balls or even playing.

If you apply The Concept while doing them, your game will receive even more benefit!

Stretching and Physical Fitness

This one is obvious. Tension in your muscles greatly limits swinging the golf club. Thirty minutes of proper stretching is FAR BETTER for your golf game than thirty minutes spent reinforcing a tense golf swing.

My recommendation is to find golf-specific stretches and build your mental game as you stretch. I also highly recommend seeking out a Titleist Performance Institute trainer and having them set you on the path to peak physical golf performance.

They are the absolute standard of physical golf training, in my opinion. If you want recommendations, please contact me and I will direct you to one in your local area.

I will address this more in the chapter entitled Health and Healing.

Meditation

Western culture doesn't know how to relax. Learning the art of relaxation would be the most beneficial thing you could do for your golf game. A quiet mind leads to a quiet body.

We are so obsessed in this culture with the pursuit of something, be it money or notoriety or some goal, that our minds don't have an opportunity to be quiet. Just watch people in traffic or in the mall.

Be meditative in your stillness. Relax and enjoy your solid foundation. Feel the connection that you have with the ground and breath deeply. Notice your breath. Feel it.

Meditation is a practice and technique that can produce fabulous results in many areas of life, and is particularly effective for golfers.

A quiet, clear mind that is able to focus provides the perfect garden for The Concept to grow.

This subject also deserves a study separate from this book so I only touch on it here. My advice would be to learn the art of meditation and implement it into your life in whatever way you can. It may seem like something reserved for "New Age" types, but I can assure you it is not.

I have a friend who has written a delightful book on meditation that will give you a solid foundation to begin and understand the practice and the benefits of it. His name is Alex Mill and the book is *Meditation And Reinventing Yourself*.

Vision and Eye Exercises

Considering that The Concept teaches that all that matters is contact, it will be very helpful in applying The Concept if you can actually see the contact occur.

I didn't see the club hit the ball once in my life until I started seeking to see it.

Even after The Epiphany, it took some time for me to train myself to be undistracted by all the things that could divert my eyes from the ball through impact.

I found that focusing on a specific dimple on the ball as Retief Goosen suggested, helped to get my eyes more locked in than they had been previously, but it still took a great deal of practice for me to maintain that focus through the swing.

Pro golfers will often utilize vision drills such as moving a tee around and back and forth in front of them while maintaining focus on the point of the tee. This type of drill can be a very effective to improve vision, but let's do something that will translate more directly to what works. Use a golf ball. Put a dot on a dimple. Focus on that.

I will often have a golf ball with me so that I can practice this vision drill when I am waiting for something. I also add a mental aspect to the drill as I bring love and intent to staying focused on that single dimple. I am not just working on my vision. I am also working on my ability to focus clearly. This has been great for both my game and my eyes!

Singing

There is no activity in the world better for your soul and body simultaneously than singing.

I know it sounds silly, but research it. The benefits of singing are far reaching and the beauty of it is that you don't even have to be good! Of course, being good may help if you are singing with a lot of people around.

The best kind of singing to do is the kind that is done for the pure enjoyment of it and is free from judgment of any kind. This particular kind of singing has always been difficult for me until I discovered a fantastic practice.

I now sing with my ears plugged or covered. It completely changes the experience. I have a pair of headphones that fit snugly to my head and block out almost all sound. They have no wires, but are not what we would refer to today as wireless. They serve only one purpose. They keep me from hearing the external sound I produce and judging the quality (or lack thereof) of that sound.

This is exactly the same as the No-Target practice approach that I use on the driving range. Again, if you eliminate the standard by which you judge, then judging becomes infinitely more difficult.

This practice has done more in the last few months to improve my singing than all the practice I had done in the previous twenty years. It has really helped my golf, as well!

Writing and Reading

I know these words are usually stated in the reverse order, but I said it this way on purpose to create a sense of what is more valuable.

Writing this book has provided more clarity of mind for me than any other thing I have done in my life. The meaning of The Concept has become crystal clear and I have felt it fill every recess of my mind.

Reading about it has done the same, although not to the same degree.

My friend Mark and I notice that every time we have conversations about The Concept, we have renewed enthusiasm to play golf and tennis, and we also seem to play them at much higher levels of performance and enjoyment than we had become accustomed in previous years.

One of the unforeseen bonuses of writing about golf and studying the psychology around it is that I can take long breaks from playing now and return to the game as though I was never away.

Weeks and even months have passed between rounds as I have worked on developing The Concept and coaching others in it, but when I return to the course following these periods I make pure contact!

I always work on some writing related to The Concept or read some of the things I have already written before I play golf now. It serves to get my mind in the right place and helps me have an enjoyable time playing. Give it a try!

"Last night I lost the world,
and gained the universe."

C. Joybell C.

Chapter 11

The Case against Caring

You care too much. You really do.

Even as you're reading this, you may be thinking to yourself, "This doesn't apply to me." Yes, it does.

The Samurai are almost universally regarded as the greatest warriors ever because they freed themselves from fear and caring. They "died" before going into battle.

My good friend and associate Steve Chandler loves the title of Warrior because it depicts the Samurai. They have courage because that is all that is left for them. There can be nothing other than courage in the complete absence of fear.

A great friend of mine who is also an exceptional golfer once told me that this single thought, die before going into battle, has freed him to accomplish things he never otherwise could have accomplished and has allowed him to have conversations and experiences he otherwise never would have had.

The Samurai could teach us a lot about how to approach golf more effectively. Theirs is the ultimate example of fully embracing The Concept. They have absolutely no attachment to any outcome. They literally do not care and it frees them to wield their swords with absolute relaxation and precision. They do not flinch.

What if we became like the Samurai on the golf course? How could the club we wield be like their swords? How could not caring about any outcome allow us to be relaxed and free?

Everything about the golf swing improves when we are relaxed. One of the most obvious and visible signs of a relaxed relationship to the golf club is in what happens immediately at and through contact. This is known as the release.

The release. This could not be more appropriately named! This is where we let go.

For some fabulous examples of great releases by tour players, look at Freddy Couples and Vijay Singh. I know Vijay probably cares a little more than Freddy does, but he sure is relaxed through his release.

I once watched Vijay hit drivers for 30 minutes on the range and I think the only thing he was working on that day was relaxation through impact. It was a thing of beauty!

Freely releasing the golf club after creating contact is a function of not being attached to result. If you are not tension-free in your follow-through after striking the golf ball, then you can be certain that you are attached to the outcome of the shot or where the ball goes.

If your only goal was to produce contact, then once the contact has taken place, your goal has been achieved! What can we do when we have achieved a goal? We can relax.

When a sprinter crosses the finish line, what do they do? They completely relax, exhale, and allow themselves to slow to a stop. They do not maintain tension past the finish line. They are finished with the race. It is over.

It is the same with the contact of a golf ball. Create the contact, then exhale and enjoy it. You have achieved your purpose. There is no need to utilize tension to guide the club into a position.

Contrary to popular belief, or at least popular practice, talking to the ball once it is moving is not going to change where it goes! By the way, if you're watching someone else play golf, talking to the ball will have even less value and may be very annoying. Just saying.

Likewise, leaning, guiding, and manipulating the club after contact will create the same sort of non-result!

We truly can only do our best and, once done, we can change nothing about what we did. It is in the past.

Look at PGA Tour pros. Even the ones who have really unconventional (polite) swings, like Kenny Perry or Jim Furyk, look very relaxed with their follow-throughs once they have contacted the ball.

This may seem counterintuitive, but the greatest gift you can offer your own future is to not care a thing about it.

Released from having to live up to your expectations, your future is now free to work out much more in line with what you desire!

To help explain that more clearly, I present the following:

Worrying **in the present** about the past and the future creates tension. NOT HELPFUL.

Being FULLY aware of and LOVING the present eliminates worry and tension. VERY HELPFUL

When you get to the point that you TRULY only care about the contact you create (and you can't pretend because your physiology knows when you're lying), you will start creating results you never dreamed possible.

If you care about something other than contact, you will surely experience doubt and fear which will in turn create tension, causing you to flinch prior to or at impact with the golf ball.

What is flinching? It's "a quick, nervous movement of the face or body as an instinctive reaction to surprise, fear or pain." It is not massive, useless, destructive, unwanted tension.

Flinching is not a habit golfers hope to develop. And yet, they will harbor thoughts in their minds that will make it impossible for their bodies NOT TO FLINCH!

Besides creating a scenario where flinching is almost certain to occur, caring produces many other unwanted circumstances.

Caring shows a clear attachment to outcome or results. Attachment to outcome creates an overwhelming need to focus on producing that outcome.

Focus on result hinders learning.

Focus on result hinders action. Here is a short list of other things that focusing on results does:

- Adds tension
- Creates the scenario for failure
- Stops creativity
- Creates the desire to "guide" or 'force"
- Brings judgment
- Creates panic
- Invites fear

When we care too much (or at all) about achieving a specific outcome, we are very likely to try to protect those results from possible challenges.

As it applies to golf, we can look at circumstances that arise when the shot we choose to play can be determined by our surroundings.

In the past, I spent a great deal of time trying to avoid trouble. I have even seen tips in golf publications recommending that we should find the trouble and then avoid it!

There is simply no comparison between the effectiveness of aiming toward a place you want the ball to go, and aiming away from a place you don't want it to go!

The ball will nearly always head directly for the spot we told ourselves we wouldn't hit it!

The science and psychology behind why this occurs is illustrated in many areas of life. If I tell you not to think of elephants, what do you think of? Elephants. Right! This is unquestioned and is easily understood when presented to you.

Studies have shown that the subconscious mind, much like a young child, finds the word "don't" to be somewhat meaningless and pays no attention to it.

Show a toddler something they shouldn't touch and, guess what? Let the touching begin!

Our minds work the same way! Why then would we ever seek out the danger and then try not to hit the ball toward the picture in our minds?

The far superior and effective approach is to find the spot you WANT to hit the ball and aim there with conviction and love. Yes, love.

As discussed earlier, the addition of love to shot selection and execution is of incredible value. Set up with yourself aligned to the ideal target and then leave it alone. Don't think about it. Don't continue to look at it and wish and hope that your ball will find its way there.

If the process is correct and your focus remains on creating pure contact, the ball will have no choice as to where it ends up. The ball cannot rebel against circumstances like an angry child. It doesn't have the ability to choose!

Speaking of children, I have two sons. One has unbelievable hand-eye coordination and could excel enormously at almost anything he does. He is good at golf, basketball, football, tennis, and other sports. He is already, at the age of 13, nearly a world-class Ping-Pong player and will soon arrive at the point where he will never lose to me again.

He has only one thing that holds him back from high-level success in any of these sports. He cares. A lot. He is constantly under the stress of wondering whether he is doing things the right way. He has an enormous fear of being wrong. I'm pretty sure he got this from his dad.

He hasn't yet learned that caring so much is not a great option. We're working on getting him past that a little earlier than I did!

Permission

One thing you can do that will very powerfully relieve you from the unneeded stress and pressure of caring too much is to give yourself PERMISSION to fail miserably!

If you happen to hit a ball out of bounds, will it honestly change anything about your life? No. But your reaction to it might. And it WILL reveal a tremendous amount about you when that reaction goes on full public display and you find yourself needing to replace a pair of $200 Oakley sunglasses. Speaking hypothetically, of course.

Giving yourself absolute and unconditional permission to hit "bad shots" will greatly reduce the likelihood that you will ever hit them!

Don't be surprised when you do not achieve perfection. There has never been a perfect golfer and there never will be.

The only thing that occurs when you demand perfection of yourself is that you bring fear into the equation, which sabotages your capacity to love. Enjoyment of the process will force out fear, release you from the tension created by fear, and will help to create results without any focus on results.

Quite often, as I was becoming familiar with applying The Concept to my golf game, I would get myself entirely relaxed and tension free and create a fantastic contact. This would result in a great outcome and suddenly my mind would re-engage into its more natural "Caring About Result" mode.

This creates "The Curse of the Follow-up Shot."

You will find that it is nearly impossible to do it twice in a row until you understand that there is no twice in a row. You are not seeking to create a series of good shots. You are hitting just one. This one.

If the last shot is still in your head it will create expectation of some kind, either positive or negative, but both will lead you off the track of focusing on and loving the one that is now.

Not caring allows you to narrow your focus and remain in that focus.

Sean Foley, the incredibly gifted golf teacher who has changed the games of many of the world's best for the better, has created or at least participated in the creation of a training aid that I think every golfer should have. This training aid helps with narrowing focus.

It is a club with a head the size of the golf ball. It, by itself, will make a difference in your game as it serves to FORCE you to make great contact to even get the ball to fly. This club will probably sell very well until Sean is no longer coaching Tiger Woods. That is a shame. Because whether or not he coaches Tiger, this product has enormous value for what it can help you learn.

You must stay entirely focused on the ball to hit it with a club head the size of a saltine cracker. If you were to couple that training aid with a firm understanding of The Concept you would change your game entirely.

There are those who are naturally less caught up in over-caring and are therefore quite relaxed. This predisposition makes them far more likely to produce good contact and they may not understand, or even know, that other people don't have that same ability.

I became aware that all people didn't share the same abilities when I was 20 years old.

I come from a fairly musical family and we would often sing around the piano at home and in various church and community groups when I was young.

Our friends all seemed to be able to sing as well so it came as something of a shock to me when a friend of mine told me that I could sing and I ought to do something with it. "What do you mean, I can sing? Can't everyone?" was my response to him.

Well, as it turns out, everyone can't sing, as has been evidenced by Russell Crowe's somewhat puzzling appearance in the recent movie version of the highly acclaimed and beloved Broadway musical *Les Miserables*.

Which brings me to another observation: Oh, the hostility of those who cannot stomach the possibility that all of their opinions are not shared by others!

In this age of social media and Internet commentary, many people have been given a voice who otherwise would have had none. Many of those people should never have been given that voice!

Should you ever dare to challenge the opinion of an Internet comment poster, BEWARE! They can be vicious in their replies. They care WAY TOO MUCH about everything!

My observation from this experience as it applies to golf is this: please don't allow yourself the disservice of being so defensive about the ideas that you may hold as truth that you immediately cast away all other options and ideas.

The gift of testing and experimenting with an open mind, free of judgment, is immeasurably valuable to your experience of the game of golf and life as a whole.

I don't want to stray from the central message. I will say it in as many ways as necessary so that it becomes part of you: **You would be better served to care less about golf than you currently do.**

Please do not misinterpret. This is NOT pretending not to care like a flippant teenager who tells his parents, "I'm getting a piercing and a tattoo, and I don't care what you think!"

That behavior, by the way, more likely indicates a very high level of caring by showing that I care SO much about what you think that I will shape my entire behavior to be the opposite. It's a bit of a shame more people can't seem to understand this.

No. This is actual "peaceful, accepting of any outcome because I will still be ok" kind of not caring. It is real and it is infinitely effective.

Since the beginning of time we have been taught, literally bullied, into placing too much value into every little thing we do. We will be exposed as lacking humanity if we don't care to the depth of our souls about everything.

If we look at the greatest performers, not just in sport, but in practically all things, we find that they all had at least one thing in common. They were able to detach themselves from the feeling and pressure of having to do something and were driven by the wanting to do something.

It was the love of their craft that created the circumstances where they succeeded time and time again, not the fear of some possible failure!

When we see someone who is brilliant at something and produces at an extremely high level, we often refer to those people as machines. He is a machine, we'll say, as though it is some unattainable personal trait that a select few are born with, allowing them to succeed at a much higher rate than others.

What is it that makes machines different? They take specific action over and over again without variation to the action, thereby producing nearly identical results. They also lack something that humans have. They don't feel. They have no fear. They don't care.

Some people will be concerned that acting like a machine will give up too much of their humanness.

If holding onto being human ruins the experience of being human, then take a break from it until you can achieve the results that humans like to measure themselves by. Then you can return to acting like an emotional human and revel in it for a bit.

After winning each championship, Michael Jordan would allow himself a few hours of enjoyment before turning back into the machine that created all his success.

Even though I love the song, I am not saying that we ought to "Be Like Mike." But we can at least learn something from him that helps us be what we want to be in our world.

No conversation about the value of not caring could be complete without at least mentioning my Aunt Helen.

Aunt Helen is no longer with us, but she was for a long time and taught us a lot while she was here.

Aunt Helen's life can be clearly divided into two parts. There was the part that existed before she fell off the horse and sustained the brain injury and then there was the part that existed after that fall.

Before the fall, she was very conscientious and immaculately neat and clean. Her house was spotless and her days planned out. She dressed very well and took her appearance very seriously.

She also wasn't the nicest person be around all the time.

That all changed the day the horse Helen was riding decided he didn't want her on his back anymore. He threw her off and she landed on her head, sustaining a severe concussion and bleeding on the brain that lead to some brain damage.

It was months before she could clearly communicate, but when she finally did leave the hospital, she did so as a different person. She was now a person who just didn't care.

If her house was a mess, it didn't bother her. If someone showed up late, oh well. If she had horse manure on her boots, it was fine. If there was no time to take a shower today, well, she could take a bath tomorrow.

She also became very nice.

I think the part of her brain that contained judgment and worry and fear got removed during the surgery.

The most interesting part of her transformation occurred when she realized she needed to find a new way to earn a living, as she wasn't capable of doing what she had done before the accident.

She did the logical thing for someone who bathed sporadically and was always working in the barn. She became an Avon Lady!

She didn't just sell Avon. She sold Avon to people who would never have considered buying it before she came around. She sold it to basically everyone in the neighborhood and set all sorts of sales records.

She was the best Avon Lady in Trenton and she didn't care a lick about what she looked like or how anyone thought of her. She was fantastic and I miss her.

And to me, Aunt Helen is the greatest argument against caring being something that is necessary and helpful. Learn from her example and your golf game, playing partners, and family members will thank you for it!

"SIMPLICITY IS ULTIMATELY A
MATTER OF FOCUS."

ANN VOSKAMP

Chapter 12

Mushrooms and Dandelions

I grew up in a very small town in southeastern Ontario in Canada.

The summers were short and very long-awaited after what seemed to be endless winters of snow and ice and freezing cold.

When spring finally did arrive, as it did every year, it brought with it gorgeous, lush, green grass and forested hills with colorful plants and flowers everywhere.

Yes, our springs and summers, although only a few months long, were beautiful and fun. As kids, we went outside when the last snow was gone and didn't come back in again until school started in the fall!

Our family yard was somewhere between one and two acres in size and needed to be mowed to be enjoyed. That task fell to our push-mower and me and took an enormous amount of time.

I got through it by singing 80's music at the top of my lungs (which the neighbors found both entertaining and annoying, as I have been told in my later years) and by looking forward to the running about and playing that I would be able to do in that vast expanse of yard once it was nicely manicured.

My best friend, Brian, and I would play catch, tag, lawn darts, and whatever else we could come up with in that yard until the sun went down nearly every day.

Inevitably, a few days after mowing, the yard would fill up with dandelions and mushrooms, which I thought were beautiful and lots of fun (I'll tell you why in a moment) but my dad found them to be unpleasant and frustrating and spent lots of time trying to get rid of them. We never could get rid of them, however, and I have finally arrived at a place in life where I understand the benefit of our futility!

Brian wasn't always around or able to play so I had to come up with other ways to entertain myself, and the yard full of weeds (dandelions) and fungus (mushrooms) would often provide the perfect forum for that entertainment!

I would take whatever golf club I could find and spend what seemed to be hours taking the heads off the dandelions and mushrooms with it.

Some of the best swings—as though some are better than others! —I ever made with a golf club probably occurred in that back yard with no one around to see them.

I would stand over the target of my forthcoming violence and focus on it and nothing else. There was only one goal: removal of that little thing in front of me with a perfect stroke! I would then take the club back and put it into a position that would allow me to very accurately swing it downward along a nice shallow arc and perfectly remove the head of the offending growth.

Hundreds, if not thousands, of those little plants met their doom at the hands of whatever junky golf club I could find in the basement. I loved doing it. And I was pretty good at it.

Why was it so easy to knock the head off a mushroom?

I have come to understand why in the last couple of years more so than ever before in my life.

There are actually some clear psychological (and therefore physiological) reasons that cleanly taking the top off of a mushroom with a golf club is much easier than knocking a ball off the top of a tee with that same golf club.

The first psychological reason behind this difference is that I had no agenda with the mushroom. I didn't have any perceived place in the yard where I needed to propel it in order to measure my comparative ability with other mushroom strikers.

Because of that fact, my attention was focused only on the mushroom itself and not on what I needed to do with it.

A second reason these swings were free of tension and judgment is that I had not yet been instructed in the proper technicalities of how one should swing the club on a perfect plane in order to strike the mushroom and perfectly remove the head from it with the tool I had in my hands, which at this time was a golf club.

This allowed me again to focus only on the act of striking the mushroom with the golf club and left me free from the tension that would be created by believing that I had to do it a specific way for it to be right.

A third reason is that no one was around at the time to ridicule me in the event that I didn't strike the mushroom well and in the manner that "professional mushroom top removers" would do it.

Since The Epiphany (see chapter 6), I have shifted the way I view a golf ball sitting on a tee in front of me. Now, I see it much the same as I would see one of those mushrooms in my yard back in Trenton. As a matter of fact, without The Epiphany, it would never have occurred to me to see the ball the way I do now.

We were discussing this very analogy on the most recent Brothers' Golf Trip to Flagstaff, Arizona where we were playing some of the best courses in the state. One of these was The Canyon Course at Forest Highlands. This course is magnificently designed on a spectacular piece of real estate and is highlighted by the signature 14th hole. This hole is a very picturesque par 3 with an island green that you hit down to from a nicely elevated tee.

I had been striking the ball quite well that day (much better than I had on previous golf outings with my wife's brothers) and one of them was asking how I was doing it as we climbed the stairs to the tee box of that par 3.

On that particular day, the hole was playing 165 yards with little or no wind.

As I stepped up to the ball, I explained to Ryan and Jeff how I used the memory of knocking the heads off of mushrooms to bring my focus entirely to the striking of the golf ball and out of the very complex realm of technical golf thoughts.

"I simply put the club into a position from which I can make pure contact between the center of the clubface and a specific dimple on the golf ball and then make the swing to produce that contact."

No agenda. No manipulation. Only the joy of pure contact.

Once contact is made, the ball will go where it will go.

No amount of visualizing, wishing, hoping, or manipulation will force the ball to go anywhere other than where it became destined to go at the instant the clubface came into contact with it.

The contact that was made on that particular swing was pure and tension free. The ball flew on a perfect arc through the clear mountain air and landed a couple of yards past the flag, took one hop and proceeded to spin back, tracking toward the hole until…plunk…it disappeared into the bottom of the cup. A hole-in-one!

The celebration was loud and long! We raced around shouting and high-fiving like junior high kids. My voice may have sustained permanent damage!

Neither Jeff nor Ryan had ever had a hole-in-one or even seen one in the thousands of rounds of golf they had played. I hadn't had one since I was 18. To make it even more magical, my father in law was on the trip with us and had predicted that morning that one of the boys was going to have an ace!

That was as pure a contact as I could have made on the ball and I give all credit to the mushrooms and dandelions that once riddled my back yard! It was also a great validation of The Concept!

Obviously, that type of result doesn't happen on every shot, but that pure contact can be created very regularly by simply having my focus be on the only thing that matters in golf: CONTACT! Love that, and everything else will fall into place!

It doesn't help to have my focus on some technicality of a perceived correct golf swing.

It doesn't help to be visualizing the flight of the ball as I am trying to make pure contact with it.

It doesn't help to be manipulating the clubface with tension to try to make the ball fly a specific direction.

And what may help least of all is trying to hit the ball HARD.

If none of these things help, then it would serve me best not to do them.

Thank you, Mushrooms and Dandelions, for teaching me how simple and joyful this game of golf can be.

LOVE THE ACTION, LOVE THE RESULT.

Chapter 13

Don't Trust. LOVE!

This book is, in its simplest form, intended to break with the establishment of golf instruction at a foundational level.

And so it is necessary for me to reference a teaching which has become so much a part of the game that it's referenced by nearly every teacher, every television analyst, and every golfer trying to impart his wisdom to his fellow golfers both during weekend rounds and on the range. (By the way, one of the most cringe-worthy events I or you or anyone will ever be party to is the friend who takes it upon himself to teach his friend how to improve his golf game.)

The teaching I am clearly referring to is this:

YOU MUST TRUST YOUR SWING.

I can already feel the controversy this is stirring up inside you as you read this. "Surely, he isn't going to try to tell me that this idea is wrong!"

Let me first say that I understand where the idea comes from. I understand that through years of practicing golf instruction, teachers of the game have helped this idea evolve because they have seen benefits from it. They have seen this idea provide an additional level of comfort and relaxation and consistency to the golfer who adopts it. But it's an artificial fix that seeks to correct a surface problem.

I strongly subscribed to this idea throughout my golfing life, and put in hours and hours of work on it. After all, if I practice enough applying the techniques that I have learned through countless hours of devouring golf magazine articles and watching "Learn From the Pros" on the golf channel, have I not now been armed with the tools that will help me develop the perfect golf swing?

The endless pursuit and acquisition of tips that consistently show signs of changing my golf game for the better--should they not be deserving of reward?

I cannot count the times that I have walked off the course after a so-called "career" round and been certain that I have finally found the swing worthy of my trust, only to find that no matter how much trust I give to my swing in subsequent rounds, it still shows itself to be the fickle mistress that it is and will always be.

You see, the pro golfer has a distinct advantage over the rest of us and it lies in the very description of who he or she is; it can be summed up in one word: PRO.

Because they are compensated for what they do, pro golfers have the eight hours of every day that the rest of us spend working at something other than golf to work on their golf swings.

Endless repetition and proper instruction create mental and muscle memory that become repeatable for the pro over time. It is inevitable that we become better at doing that which we persist in doing.

Let us look for a moment at Webster's Dictionary:

Definition of TRUST

1   a : <u>assured</u> reliance on the character, ability, strength, or truth of someone   or something

b : one in which confidence is placed

2 **a** : dependence on something future or <u>contingent</u> : hope

b : reliance on future payment for property (as merchandise) delivered : <u>credit</u> <bought furniture on *trust*>

I don't know what comes up for you when you read this, but let me share a little of what comes up for me.

The first thing I notice is the amount of work involved.

I will need to develop assured reliance, placing of confidence, and dependence on someone or something that is external to myself, over which I have no control. This seems like a lot of emotional energy to me.

Second is the fact that all of that work is being placed on someone or something as it relates to FUTURE events and being contingent upon some expected or hoped-for outcome—the most telling word in the definition being HOPE!

This brings me to another common phrase—one used by high handicappers to describe their golf games: HIT AND HOPE!

Based on the definition of trust, this Hit-and-Hope approach is simply a slightly less refined version of the more accepted Trust Your Swing. Both take the possibility of happiness outside of you and place it on an unknown future.

Both require energy that is not otherwise required and lead to you become prematurely exhausted from playing a game whose purpose is to provide stress relief and joy!

Have you ever experienced what it's like to hope for something?

I remember trying out for the high school basketball team and not being able to sleep for the two days we had to wait before the final list went up. I hoped and hoped and hoped that my name would be on that list. When the list finally went up, my name was not on it.

How could that be, with all the hoping I had done? Shouldn't the hoping have created the scenario for success? No!

Performance suffers every time hope is present.

At its best, hope is distracting and tiring, and at its worst it can be absolutely exhausting and excruciating.

As Steve Chandler asks, , why add trust and belief to the equation? All they do is muddy the waters of a process that may already be complicated enough without them.

A story that effectively illustrates this principle took place in my basement while I was writing this book.

I was playing Ping-Pong with my son Carter, who was just nine at the time, and he made an observation that I will never forget. I should preface this by saying that Carter often says profound things and has been doing so since he learned how to talk, so we are careful to have something with us to write on at all times.

On this particular day, he was struggling a little with his game (he is actually quite a good Ping-Pong player, albeit with a style that is uniquely his own) and was beginning to show signs of frustration when he suddenly exclaimed "Dad, I'm not going to believe in myself anymore!"

It seemed an interesting thing for him to say and maybe even a little concerning, so I asked him what he meant by it. He responded, "When I believe in myself, I always miss the shot. But when I DON'T believe in myself, the ball always lands in!"

What a brilliant observation from such a young person. He understood that having to "believe in himself" took energy away from what he was doing and added unnecessary pressure for him to live up to!

Trusting is an investment of emotional energy that we create around a given person, thing, or circumstance. We spend time thinking and weighing our past experience with that person or thing. We ask ourselves, "Do I trust this person?" and then spend time trying to analyze and discern their behavior to determine if they are worthy of our trust.

Then, when they do something unexpected or outside of the expectation that we have set up as a standard for them to deserve our trust, we have to first deal with the shock, sadness, and emotional turmoil they have caused, then go through the entire process again to see if we are willing to reissue that trust.

Can you get so wrapped up in TRUSTING your significant other that you forget to love them?

The experience of trust is only valuable to the person who perceives it as a necessary gift that others must give them as part of their existence.

And while we're in the discussion, please beware of any company that feels a necessity to give itself a name intended to secure your trust as a consumer. Generally, if I see the word "integrity" in the name of a business, I keep shopping!

Because typically, the person obsessed with seeking the trust of others is the person least deserving of it.

Lives will be spent in an effort toward rebuilding trust after some indiscretion (real or perceived) occurs in a relationship, when that life could more usefully be spent loving, serving, and enjoying.

Now, imagine the complexity of trying to apply this process to a golf swing! Is there a possibility that your golf swing will live up to this sacred trust and never let you down? I can't make trusting my swing a necessity, because what happens when I don't?

So here's the bottom line. My request of myself, as well as anyone I coach is this:

Please do not add anything that takes away from the experience of joy around the EVENT that is golf; that is, **the feeling of pure contact as clubface connects with the ball. Love it unconditionally! The rest is purely observation.**

"BUT IF THOUGHT CORRUPTS LANGUAGE, LANGUAGE CAN ALSO CORRUPT THOUGHT."

GEORGE ORWELL

Chapter 14

Watch Your Language

This Chapter has nothing to do with cursing.

I would understand if you did curse on the golf course from time to time. Lots of people do. The word "GOLF" is often described as "the other 4-letter word!"

No. Cursing, although perhaps somewhat socially unacceptable and inappropriate in various settings, is much less damaging to your game than the language I'm referring to.

I'm also not referring to positive or negative self-talk, which can also have an impact on your experience of golf.

I am referring to language that up until now you may have viewed as helpful and instructive. I intend to illustrate for you why it is not.

There are catch phrases in golf that are so much a part of the culture of instruction that you would be hard-pressed to find any golfer from beginner to tour player who would be unfamiliar with them.

It is language that serves to create internal conflict without you ever realizing what is happening. Internal conflict creates tension. Once again, tension=not good.

One morning I took what has now become my familiar position on the range — right next to the teaching pro at my local golf course. I like to listen in and hear what is being taught and apply what I find helpful to my game.

I like this pro. I like his style and what he does for his students. He has a passion for making them better and I can see the results coming. I particularly love his consistency with having his students understand that their eyes should never leave the golf ball throughout the swing.

On this particular morning, he was working with a lady who was obviously very committed to improving her golf game. She was really working hard and doing her very best to listen and apply everything she was being taught.

She was, however, having one problem that day which seemed to be preventing her from producing results that she was pleased with. It is a common problem, and the problem upon which the very premise of this book is based.

She kept looking up prior to making contact with the golf ball.

He then gave her the famous instruction:

"Keep your head down."

And thus begins our conversation of what language needs to be eliminated or changed in order to bring love and enjoyment back to the game!

No more "keeping my head down!"

Let's look at this phrase and the kind of conflict it subconsciously creates when it is believed.

Having a need to "keep your head down" first assumes that your natural tendency and desire is to lift your head up. A competing force then must be applied to stop this natural action from occurring.

As a point of example, ask someone to help keep your head down when you are trying to lift it. No fun, is it? Can you feel the tension and conflict created?

What would work much better would be to have absolutely no desire to lift your head up in the first place, thereby eliminating the need to "keep it down!"

So much of golf instruction, which in turn becomes the commentary on golf, which is shared between all golfers worldwide, comes from language like this.

I have a pile of golf magazines on my desk, and inside each one of those magazines are several well-meaning articles defining what needs to happen in order to become a better golfer.

Each of these things in turn gets read and interpreted by an instructor, or more likely by a weekend golfer, who then takes that information to the range and tries to implement it without any help or coaching. Worse yet, that golfer attempts to share what he has "learned" with his friends.

This creates the cultural language of golf.

In most cases, neither the instructor nor the golfer is aware of the language they are using to convey these teachings or how that language impacts the psychology and physiology of what they are doing.

But language matters.

How we think about and speak about anything we do in golf (and life, for that matter) creates (and reveals) the context in which we experience that thing.

To that end, I have changed the language I use around every aspect of my golf game.

For example, I don't ever work on my "swing." Why? Because, to me, there really is no such thing as a golf swing.

Obviously, to play the game of golf, a golfer must swing the club, but to say there is "a golf swing" would be to imply that there is only one. During a round of golf, I will most likely not use the same swing twice. That's one of the reasons I don't work on my golf swing. I experiment with making different sorts of contacts between the club and the ball.

In keeping with this theme, I no longer think of the "backswing" as a "backswing." There's the action of placing the club into a position from which I can create contact between the face of the golf club and the golf ball.

And if I choose to add a mild amount of complexity to things, I will move my focus to different spots on the golf ball to create different kinds of contact. This will change both how I swing the club and the flight of the golf ball after I have created contact with it. (I will address that more later.)

It's really that simple.

Part of the experience of the application of this concept that has been so mind-boggling to me is the complete and utter relaxation I feel in the "backswing."

No longer is there tension in my hips or back or shoulders and I find myself in a very comfortable manner simply taking the club away from address at the ball and placing it at the top of my "swing."

There is no thought in doing this other than when I have arrived at the top I will allow the club to fall toward the ball so that the face of the club can make contact with the ball.

As one of my first moves in bringing language into my golf that positively affects my application of The Concept and thereby, the whole experience surrounding golf, I will no longer refer to shots as "shots." Rather, they will be referred to for what they are in the context of The Concept: Contacts.

Using the word "Contact" as the language to identify what I am doing each time I strike the golf ball with the club will help bring my mind back repeatedly to what I am actually doing in that instant, entirely free from attachment to outcome.

I am not making shots. Hitting a golf shot automatically creates attachment to the outcome of the action I am participating in. Where the ball flies is the *result* of what I am doing and should be allowed to assume its proper place in my mind.

I am Creating Contact. And the clearer I am on that fact, the purer and more joyful that contact will be!

I have a definitive sequence that I follow to give each contact its full attention and own place inside a round of golf or a practice session. One could almost view it as a mantra.

I have found this mantra to be more valuable to me than any other practice I have incorporated into my routine since The Epiphany brought me The Concept.

It is this:

CONTACT->OBSERVATION->NEXT

The simple practice of repeating this phrase has allowed each Contact with the golf ball to occupy its own space, free of judgment. There is only Contact. I bring love and joy to the action of creating that Contact.

As we have learned before, the focus and intent that comes through the desire to create pure Contact creates a space that is totally present in the instant Contact occurs. There is no awareness or concern with either past (prior to Contact) or future (where the ball goes after Contact) in that instant. There is a reason that we need coaches in our lives. They serve us by constantly reminding us what works.

We become habitual in how we exist and experience things in our own world as humans and we fail to see things in different ways. Coaches help bring us back to awareness and out of habitual living.

The movie *Dead Poet's Society*, has always had great personal meaning to me and perfectly illustrates this idea.

In the movie, Robin Williams is a teacher at a private boys' school and utilizes some very unorthodox teaching methods. At one point, he has the boys stand on desks to see how different the classroom looks from that perspective.

When I first saw this movie I didn't fully understand what he was trying to teach. I think I understand it more clearly now.

Perspective means everything to experience. Language is evidence of perspective.

If we are to look at The Concept, we will also understand that we are seeing it only from our current perception or perspective. My intent with explaining it from multiple directions is to allow you to have that change in perspective that Robin Williams was trying to give those kids.

The Concept states, "The only thing that matters is Contact!" When this is fully understood and grasped, it will have a much deeper meaning to you than it does now from just reading words on the page.

The Concept involves three mindsets as shown in the mantra above that are necessarily worth repeating:

Contact ->Observation->Next

Each of these mindsets occurs inside of its own moment.

The backswing is no longer a backswing. It is now only an action that puts the club into a position from which I can make a descending blow on the golf ball and create pure Contact.

The club is only a tool used to create that Contact. If we think of it as something that we use to hit shots, we have overstepped the boundaries of a functional definition and have created a subconscious pressure to produce a certain outcome.

The new language of golf for me is the language of The Concept. Since the only thing that matters is Contact and since that is what I love about golf, I have shifted my language accordingly.

There is no backswing. There is only the placing of the club in a position from which I can strike the ball.

There is no shot. There is only Contact. The flight of the ball is determined by Contact.

I no longer KEEP my head down. I now watch the ball.

I do not swing hard. I swing relaxed and that relaxation produces speed.

Swinging hard creates tension and actually slows clubhead speed. Relaxation relieves tension and creates speed.

I do not putt the ball. I place the putter into a position from which I can create Contact with the ball. I create Contact with a specific dimple on the back of the ball and allow it to travel where it will.

Most important, I do not keep score. I allow others to take care of that if they want to.

I do not reference anything in a way that will create turmoil or internal conflict. I cannot enjoy things as much if there is any sense of internal conflict going on within me.

Therefore, I do not speak about golf in a way that will create tension or draw me away from the love that I have for the action of creating pure Contact.

Can you see how the practice of speaking things differently creates an entirely different physiological response to those things? If you cannot yet, I invite you to go out and try it.

One of my favorite things to observe is watching what happens with a client when they simply change from thinking of the backswing as a backswing and instead think of it as the simple act of placing the club into a position from which they can create good Contact with the golf ball.

Try this thought shift for yourself. Think of it in this way and see what happens. The way you refer to things with language creates the relationship you have with those things, yet in most cases you'll be completely unaware of it. That is, until you become aware of it.

Thought creates language and language, in turn, shapes thought. How you think about golf will show up in how you speak about it and how you speak about golf will also greatly influence how you think about it.

For thirty years, I have had one underlying thought in my head, and it represents the most damaging type of language. That thought is "I can't."

This type of language has likely done more damage to my golf game than anything else.

"I can't putt." That was the language and the belief I held.

What does "I can't putt" mean? Can I hold a putter? Can I swing it? Can I hit a ball with it? Can I line it up so that I hit a ball toward the hole? Then what on earth does it mean to say that I can't putt? Of course I can putt. Everyone can.

"I can't putt" was a way for me to excuse my score. I was always able to walk off the 18th green and say to anyone willing to listen to me share commentary about my round, "Imagine how good I could be if I could putt!"

Being a bad putter does two things:

First, it creates stress around approach shots because you know you have to get the ball close to have any chance of scoring par or better on any hole. That stress and pressure creates stress and pressure on your tee shots to put the ball in a position in the fairway where you have a chance to hit a good approach shot.

So the first thing believing you're a bad putter does is put stress on every other shot you take on the golf course.

The second thing saying you're a bad putter does is provide an excuse as to why you didn't score well in any particular round. It gives you something to blame that will alleviate the necessity of accepting that you're not as good a golfer as you think or have let others think you are. It helps protect your ego from an admission of not being good enough.

It reminds me of something I did throughout all the adventures of my academic years.

I did relatively well in school. I had a very highly functioning memory and a fair ability to comprehend most everything that was taught from the time I was young all the way through college.

What I didn't do well was study. I didn't see any reason to study. As a matter of fact, I had a very distinct reason to not study which has become crystal clear to me since the moment I experienced The Epiphany.

I intentionally didn't study because it provided me the perfect excuse in the event I didn't do well on a test or in a class. I would hope to do very well, and I often did, but for those times I didn't, all I needed to do to relieve myself of the possibility that I wasn't as smart as I thought I was, was to say loudly and proudly that "I didn't study. If I had, I'm sure I would have been at the top of the class!"

I didn't see how dysfunctional this habitual behavior was at the time.

Therein lies the key to my believing I was a bad putter AND declaring it to any and all that would listen. It was in my best interest to remain a bad putter so that I would never lose the excuse as to why I didn't score better on the golf course. My previous relationship with golf would never have allowed me to let go of such an exceptional excuse!

I had a friend in school named Andrea. She was interesting and I had a very interesting relationship with her. The one thing I could never question about her, however, was how hard she worked. She studied. School was tougher for her than it was for me, but she worked at it and did well.

One day, I was trying to get her to pack up the books so she could join me for some fun thing that was going on and she said she couldn't because she had to study. I made some flippant comment that probably wasn't very kind, making fun of her need to study. She answered with something that hurt my feelings then, and remains with me today.

"Some day, you'll wish you had to work like I do." And she was right. I have had to learn those lessons later in life. And it has been hard.

Perhaps my language revealed my true character to her.

"THOUGHT CAN ORGANIZE THE WORLD SO WELL THAT YOU ARE NO LONGER ABLE TO SEE IT."

ANTHONY DE MELLO

Chapter 15

It's All Thought

Everything is easier than we think it is. It's our thinking that makes everything difficult.

Golf is the one sport where you spend most of your time thinking. Professional golfer Steve Marino said that perhaps 95% of a round of golf takes place in the head. I would say the percentage is even higher than that.

Let's say that an average round today, given the immensely slow rate of play that seems to be the new normal, is approximately four and a half hours. That is a total of 270 minutes.

Next we'll assume for the sake of this conversation that an average golfer shoots around bogey golf, which equates to 90 shots per game with each swing taking and average of two seconds. (But I can promise you that scores would drop if the swing of the average golfer actually did only take two seconds!

You may find the math on this a little shocking but using this scenario, the actual time spent swinging the golf club with the intent to create Contact with the ball in a typical round of golf is generously 180 seconds! That is a total of three minutes.

3 Minutes/270 Minutes=1%

From this very simplistic mathematical equation, we can assume that less than 1% of a round of golf is actually spent golfing! **What on earth are we doing with the other 99% of that time?**

I have a few ideas and, in keeping with the sub-text of the title of this book, I can tell you that what's going on during that time is not helping us.

When discussing this formula, I will divide golf into two parts:

- Part I: **The Event**

This is the action immediately surrounding and including the point at which the golf club contacts the ball. This is the three minutes in the equation.

- Part II: **The Experience**

This is everything external to the EVENT, and includes stretching, warming up, walking or riding, practicing, enjoying scenery, breathing fresh air, etc. This is the 270 minutes.

Once you grasp The Concept fully, the number of Contacts required for your round of golf is likely to drop dramatically, so the Event/Experience Ratio becomes even greater!

I want you to pay close attention to the following comment and ask yourself if it resonates with you.

How we think about something is everything.

No, I really mean it. How we think of something determines everything about how that thing exists for us.

For example, as discussed in the previous chapter, I used to think of the backswing in golf as "The Backswing." I don't think of it that way anymore. Consequently, it doesn't exist for me that way anymore. My relationship to the action I take before I hit a golf ball has entirely changed.

First of all, referring to it as the backswing gives it far more connection to the actual swing than it deserves. What we refer to out of habit as the backswing serves no purpose other than *TO PLACE THE CLUB INTO A POSITION FROM WHICH* one can make a descending blow and create Contact (pure Contact, if we are relaxed enough!) with the golf ball.

There is no ideal "backswing" to emulate. If there were, players like Lee Trevino, Jim Furyk, Kenny Perry, and Tommy "Two Gloves" Gainey could be working at Wal-Mart rather than making millions doing something they love!

Gravity and Other Things

I love watching golf on television from time to time and hearing what the commentators have to say, especially as it reveals how the players are thinking about what they are doing. Some are more entertaining than others, but it seems that all of them like to critique what they're seeing.

Most amateurs actually carry so much tension in their swings that they will fight against gravity. They believe so much in the necessity to manipulate the club into some perceived correct technical position that they will move it off its natural descent toward the ball.

Johnny Miller, when watching Tiger's near virtuoso performance at the 2013 Cadillac Championship at Doral, said that Tiger was using a "gravity swing" that looked so easy and relaxed it was almost as though he was just letting gravity hit the ball.

During a recent broadcast of the Honda Classic, the commentators were again talking about Tiger Woods's new, relaxed swing. Johnny Miller said to the viewers, "Folks, a really safe shot is you get the club up to the top and you almost just let gravity hit it. It is almost effortless. It is a really good way to lay up shots."

I wholeheartedly agree! But it's not just a great way to lay up shots; it's a great way to hit every shot! Quite often, we fight against gravity by trying to force the club on an unnatural path that we think is correct rather than allowing gravity to be our friend.

Don't we envy the effortless swing? Then why don't we do everything we can to embrace the principles that produce it?

Focus on Contact

Johnny Miller was having a conversation with Jack Nicklaus in the broadcast booth of that same 2013 Cadillac Championship at Doral; they were talking about Tiger having a ball in a sandy divot.

Tiger created great Contact (in fact, Gary Koch said just before he hit it, "This is all about Contact") and hit a great shot which prompted Johnny to say, "Sometimes you get in those divots and you concentrate more than you do on almost any shot, and you hit great shots a lot of times. Didn't you notice that in your career?" Jack responded by saying, "I hit one at Doral one year in a divot with a three-iron about 212 yards and I was leading by one shot, and I hit a great shot."

There was so much wisdom in that conversation that would go right by if we weren't listening closely and here is the wisdom:

EVERY SHOT IS ALL ABOUT CONTACT!

Is there a shot you will face on the golf course where Contact ISN'T the most important factor? No. Then why focus on or think about anything else? Now, let's add something to that focus: Love it.

So many people allow their eyes to move with the putter both back and through. Ben Crane tweeted that he was watching Tiger's eyes while Tiger was standing over a 10-footer for par during the Friday round of a PGA Championship. He noticed that Tiger stayed over the ball for an extra second and said that's how he knew he was putting well. Congratulations, Tiger!

Another comment made during the third hole was that it would be a good idea for Tiger to focus only on Contact while hitting a shot that was well off the back of the green to set himself up for a par save.

What I found interesting about the comment is how it was spoken without any follow-up reference or recognition of how powerful it was.

IT WOULD BE A GOOD IDEA TO FOCUS ONLY ON CONTACT ON EVERY SHOT! This IS the game of golf!

Each shot should be isolated so that in the event a tiny bit of judgment does creep in from time to time, that judgment is denied the opportunity to carry over and impact subsequent Contacts.

Ball striking is often referred to as one element of the game that is golf. I invite you to find a part of the game that doesn't involve striking the ball. There is nothing else. There is only ball striking.

As I've watched the PGA tour since I experienced The Epiphany, I've tried to identify players that most closely demonstrate that they have internalized The Concept. Those who fully understand that Contact is the only thing that matters, and love producing that contact, have specific elements in how they strike the golf ball that are visually identifiable.

The golfer who seems to most perfectly embody The Concept is Jordan Spieth. I have been obsessed with his game since I first saw him play as an amateur. Even then, I started telling people to watch his game and to take notice of something specific that he does.

His swing is not classically beautiful and contains some "technical" flaws (what a joke!) that the Konica Minolta Biz Hub camera makes clearly obvious in super slow motion.

But he also does something that anyone with a moderate level of awareness will notice. He has a distinct pause at the top of his swing.

This is the pause that teaching pros around the world try so hard to get their students to institute and emulate, but they never tell them why they should do it! Not the real reason, anyway. They can't tell them why because, for the most part, they don't know why.

That pause exists because there is no way for it not to when what we are doing is occurring in our minds in the most logical and most effective way.

When we think of putting the club into a position from which we can then create a descending blow to make contact with the ball, it will naturally create a slight pause. Simply *thinking of it this way* solves so many of the issues that golfers battle throughout their golfing lives!

Transition to "the Downswing" now occurs naturally!

"There is no backswing" and "Love the Contact!"

These are the ONLY thoughts I now have during the Event (as opposed to the Experience) of golf and they solve literally every technical issue that could arise for me!

Jordan Spieth embodies these thoughts. His mind is right. No amount of analyzing his swing with that ridiculous Biz-Hub machine will be able to explain why he will win countless events over the coming years.

Curtis Strange once said that Jordan Spieth was not going to be America's next superstar golfer because his swing couldn't produce long-lasting dominance. I often disagree with Curtis Strange, but never so much as I did when I heard him say that.

Swings don't produce dominance! No golf swing ever produced a win! It is the mind of the golfer that determines everything about what that golfer will accomplish.

Tournaments are won by single strokes. Do you think a "golf swing" is responsible for that? Of course not! That's a ludicrous notion.

I have noticed three or four golfers on the PGA tour that I think exemplify a solid relationship to the golf ball and how they contact it that will produce great results for them.

Three of the most obvious examples to me are Jordan Spieth, Hideki Matsuyama, and Jimmy Walker. They seem to watch the ball just a little longer than everyone else does. There is a reason. They want to see it. They are obsessed with contact. They understand that abandoning the focus on that relationship even $1/100^{th}$ of a second early will sabotage them!

There are others, but these are the three that stood out to me in 2012. I talked to rooms full of people about them. I told my mentor, Steve Chandler, to watch that Spieth kid. He was my new favorite and for all the right reasons. He has proven to be everything I imagined he would be. Just wait. He isn't finished.

There's something else that these and other effective golfers do between Events (Contacts) on the golf course. They remain calm. They meditate. They think about what they want to do and they enjoy doing it.

They absolutely never spend time thinking about what they don't want. Why? Because there is absolutely no valuable purpose behind it!

What if we utilized our time on the course between Contacts only to visualize what we wanted and never allowed ourselves to think of what we didn't want? Honestly, who walks around thinking about things they don't want? After all, that is a fairly unimaginative use of the imagination, isn't it?

The original title of this book was "**IT'S NOT ABOUT THE NUMBER**." That title drew attention to a very specific thing that we do when we golf or do anything. We make things "about the number." It doesn't help.

How do we measure golf? Golf is a sport more consumed with and defined by numbers than any other game on earth. Everything is measured in scores and statistics.

How could I have the audacity to claim that It's Not about the Number?

I claim that because making it about the number creates a mental culture that exists in the mind of each individual golfer that has them constantly judging themselves. I prefer to leave judgment out. Things work much better that way.

"Until you make the unconscious conscious, it will direct your life and you will call it fate."

C.G. Jung

Chapter 16

Health and Awareness

No discussion of golf is complete without mentioning health and the huge role it plays in both your enjoyment of the sport and your ability to play it. Health is routinely overlooked and undervalued by amateurs and we are often completely unaware of our own health and how powerfully it impacts our thoughts on both a conscious and sub-conscious level.

I named this chapter Health *and Awareness* because I believe that good health cannot be achieved or maintained without awareness, and awareness itself is definitely something worthy of more of our awareness.

This chapter isn't meant to give you lots of advice on health. Rather, it's meant to help you realize that our minds and the ability we have to choose play enormous roles in how healthy we are.

I do not want to offer you training and fitness advice, rather I want you to be more aware of the value of engaging someone who can. It is a small action to reach out to someone who can suggest simple ways to create positive change in your life.

Small and simple choices can entirely alter the way we feel, live, and play.

Awareness can be the answer to so many simple problems and challenges. The answer is almost always easier than we anticipate it will be.

Take The Concept, for example. It is so simple and its benefits so far-reaching that it makes no sense for me not to apply it. And yet, I will forget repeatedly to apply it to the most immediate circumstances in my life. This forgetfulness could occur out of habit or simply because of a less-active awareness center in my brain.

The Concept helps to clear our minds and find the answer to the WHY beneath the WHY. The Concept also helps dramatically with the reduction, if not elimination, of tension that exists in us because of the thoughts we're thinking.

Bad health can do more to promote bad thinking than perhaps any other condition. Experiencing physical pain and discomfort can literally overrun the mind with misery and despair. On top of that, bad thinking will promote further bad health in many ways.

Awareness of these simple facts can be the catalyst to a life change!

In the months prior to The Epiphany, I was experiencing severe discomfort in my wrist and collarbone. The wrist injury had occurred a year earlier while playing golf in Canada and hadn't really improved much and had become chronic. I blamed the pain in my collarbone on being a side-sleeper, but had no way of really being sure. As it turns out, I was wrong about both injuries.

I also had mild injuries to my back and neck, which had me seeing my chiropractor from time to time, but those injuries were not nearly as debilitating as the other two. I honestly thought that I would have to give up golfing, whether I wanted to or not.

Two or three months prior to The Epiphany, I had spoken with the pro at my local driving range to see if she had any idea what could be done with the specific physical problems I was experiencing. She recommended a physical therapist that worked on golf related injuries. I never went. Golf was on the way out for me anyway and the pain from injury provided one more reason for us to part.

Then came The Epiphany, and along with it, a renewed love for golf. Hopefully, the injuries wouldn't keep me from enjoying this rebirthed relationship!

A very interesting thing happened in the days following my reunion with golf. I changed my grip to relieve pressure on my wrist and then didn't really think about anything related to the injuries again.

Within a week or two, they were totally gone! How did that happen?

The tension I had been carrying to protect myself from the pain of my supposed injuries was actually contributing to their prolonged existence and may have been the cause of them in the first place!

The Concept had actually become my healer!

By eliminating my attachment and worry surrounding the past and future, my mind was freed from the thoughts that brought tension into my life. This freedom translated into a relaxed swing that actually helped my range of motion and corrected the things that were misaligned and inflamed.

Raising my level of awareness around what was really causing my pain allowed me to release that tension and let my body heal itself. Realizing that this didn't relate just to golf and physical injuries was the next step I took toward greater freedom from tension!

The full ramifications of this discovery cannot be covered in this book. That is a discussion for another time and another forum, but a fantastic discussion it is, indeed!

Muscular injuries were not the only things that were plaguing me at the time of The Epiphany. I was also experiencing several other health problems that were keeping me up at night and greatly impairing the amount of joy I was experiencing on a daily basis.

I was not breathing well and my horrid allergies were ruining any chance I ever had at a good night's sleep. My energy was low and my desire to do things that required either action or concentration was even lower.

As it related to these issues, The Concept served me in an entirely different way than it had with golf. At least, I thought it was different at the time. I now realize it was exactly the same.

All the time I was spending applying The Concept to my golf game led to me practicing the principle of detaching myself from the future and the past and focusing on what I could love and connect with in the moment. This provided clarity for me to see things I had not seen before.

The Concept opened up the part of my mind that contained good judgment!

One of the first results of that was to consider that I wasn't feeling good and there must be something I could do about it. My new found ability to step out of the fear that I had something permanently wrong with me that couldn't be treated led me to ask around to see if anyone knew someone who could help with my "unique" set of health problems

That is when I was introduced to Randy Grant.

I am not the only golfer who knows Randy. As a matter of fact, Randy is one of the most well-known nutritionists in the golf world.

He has helped many members of the PGA Tour, including Major winners, overcome health problems that had seemed insurmountable. He is also the preferred nutritionist for the European Tour and for many other players around the world.

His expertise isn't limited only to golfers; he has also worked with many professional sports teams in the major sports leagues.

.

When I met with Randy, I figured that if he could help all those professional athletes who had unlimited options, he could certainly help me!

Well, help he did! After 30 minutes of sitting with him and having him examine my blood under a microscope and fully question me on all the symptoms I was having, he recommended a few supplements for me.

His company provides supplements that utilize enzymes to address many very common health problems that otherwise are considered untreatable or, when they are treatable, require a battery of medications.

Within a few short weeks, most of the problems I had been experiencing were gone, and I no longer even think about them.

The reason I love Randy Grant and his nutritional company is that they exemplify The Concept so perfectly.

They are invested in finding the absolute root of their clients' problems and bringing as much love and focus to solving those problems as they possibly can.

I have already mentioned some things in other chapters that can greatly contribute to a healthy, happy life. Test them. Do a yoga class. Practice breathing and meditation. Find Randy Grant (I can help you with that) or someone like him. Invest in yourself and reap the rewards, for they are incredible!

Embrace the simplicity of choice! So much less is required to make a difference than we possibly imagine. Your golf game will love you for making the simple effort. More importantly, YOU will love you for it!

An application of The Concept and a heightened level of awareness will help produce a clear and effective mind. I believe that all health, either good or bad, stems from conditions that exist in the mind and will therefore be greatly served by bringing that mind more of our love and attention.

Be aware. Let go of tension. Embrace The Concept.

"I IMAGINE THAT THE INTELLIGENT PEOPLE ARE THE ONES SO INTELLIGENT THAT THEY DON'T EVEN NEED OR WANT TO LOOK 'INTELLIGENT' ANYMORE."

CRISS JAMI

Chapter 17

Commitment and Certainty

You have often, no doubt, heard how important it is to be "committed to your shot" in golf. It is constantly being referenced in golf telecast commentary and is part of virtually every teaching method in golf instruction. It's good advice, too. Commitment is an absolutely necessary quality to enjoy a great relationship with golf. The way we see commitment, however, can sometimes present challenges.

Often, the way we perceive commitment in golf can require over-commitment. Have you ever felt like you have "over-committed" yourself to anything in your life? How do you feel in the presence of over-commitment? Do you feel at peace? Do you feel comfortable and confident? Not likely.

This is the situation that you create for yourself when you commit to a golf "shot" or a golf swing. It is too much to commit to. It takes years of training and practice. It includes too many variables. It takes muscle memory. Some pros can commit to a golf "shot" and others cannot. They aren't ready yet. The reason? It encompasses too much. It is too big.

This type of over-commitment results in standing over the ball without any feelings of peace, confidence, or comfort. This is not a successful approach to commitment.

The key to success in commitment is to narrow its focus. Bring it down to something that is manageable, even enjoyable. A complete shot? That can be daunting. Contact? That is something I can work with.

I have referenced this earlier in this book. I don't think about hitting a shot. I am not even hitting shots in golf, I am creating contacts. To commit to a complete shot would require me to take responsibility for something over which I have no control as it is occurring. That is to have influence over an inanimate object as it flies through the air or bounds along the ground.

My ability to influence the outcome of a golf "shot" ends the moment the ball has left the face of the club. Therefore, my commitment is limited to the creation of contact. In this, I am enormously enthusiastic and committed!

You may think this is simply semantics and that it makes no difference whether or not I refer what I am doing as creating contact or hitting a shot. I suggest you try applying this simple shift in perception. Think of the two differently. Practice committing to both contact and a shot and see the difference between them.

How you think about something is tremendously influential and important to how that thing occurs to you. The moment I stopped committing to a golf "shot" and instead began committing to "contact" was the moment my entire golf game changed.

When you change the way you think about something, you change the relationship you have to that thing and, consequently, change the actions that you take with respect to that relationship.

I want all the emotional energy that I have available during a round of golf to be dedicated and committed to the event that is golf and that is the creation of contact.

Pure commitment is the elimination of alternative options. My friend and phenomenal Success and Performance Coach, Christopher Dorris does an excellent job of demonstrating commitment in his analogy of jumping off a cliff into the water below. He refers to it as being "All In." When you jump off a cliff, your option of NOT jumping has left you. Read his book. Listen to his audio. They're fantastic.

There is irony in the fact that it requires MORE mental energy to avoid commitment than it does to be committed. Commitment is a decision. Once the decision is made the energy around what I am going to do is now committed. Waffling and indecision are exhausting! We often don't recognize this truth.

Indecision, or fear of committing, seems to be an instinctual behavior.

My favorite episode of Seinfeld contains George's realization that every instinct he had in life was wrong and leads him to decide that he would now do The Opposite. George wasn't alone in his instincts! We could all be served by choosing to do the opposite of our instincts in most cases!

When you stand over the ball and question what you are doing, that questioning creates openings for disasters to sneak in.

Commitment is required in putting. Thoughts will naturally come into your head questioning your commitment. This is human nature. Let them pass. They are meaningless. They hold no power unless you give them power. They are untrue.

Thoughts come to challenge your commitment. They do not serve you. Breathe. Return to your commitment. True commitment cannot occur in the presence of attachment to outcome because when you are attached to outcome, your mind cannot be present.

Resisting a well-founded commitment creates a scenario for certain failure. If certain failure is what you want, then by all means, question your commitments. Questioning commitments adds layers of complication and tension to the application of those commitments.

That complication and tension will have you sweating over three footers. There was a point in Tiger Wood's career where he had made an incomprehensible 2000 putts in a row that were three feet or shorter in distance.

Commitment requires clarity and thrives in its presence. What do I really want to do? What is the action I want to take? How do I experience commitment? What is my relationship to commitment? How does that relationship show up when I'm standing over the golf ball? Am I aware?

Can we please stop pretending that how we say something is not important? How we say something reveals everything about what that thing means to us! Our relationship to the things or people we speak of is revealed in the language we use around those things!

Being committed is a valuable quality, but it has a partner which may be the most valuable of all personal traits that anyone could have with respect to specific action. That partner is CERTAINTY.

Certainty is not the same as rightness. Rightness exists only in the face of being challenged. Certainty stands on its own. I can be certain of what I am doing without there being having to be any competing idea. Rightness, on the other hand, requires that there be a wrong.

Certainty is evidence of a high level of self-esteem. The need to be right is indicative of a low level of self-esteem.

Understanding the value of certainty helps us understand what has happened with Tiger Woods. Tiger used to live in a world in which he was the only resident. His certainty was unparalleled. There was never any question of right or wrong for Tiger Woods. There was only certainty. That is no longer the case. How is the new world of uncertainty working out for him?

Of all the moments in a round of golf where the value of certainty is most evident is while standing over a short putt. Putting is easier for younger people because they haven't built in the mechanism to question themselves. Putting is more specific and immediately identifiable in its feedback than any other shot in golf. Standing over a short putt in the face of the judgment that could occur upon missing that short putt makes it the least desirable shot in golf. It is filled with expectation.

Isn't it interesting that the presence of expectation makes commitment more challenging?

Every place that fear and self judgment create tension that sabotages or disrupts an action is a place that would be immeasurably benefited by the application of the Concept.

You've heard it said, but not heard it at this exact moment in your life. So whether you've heard it in the past is completely irrelevant and until you get that, your mind is creating a barrier to progression.

Certainty is creative in nature. Rightness is protective. Certainty can be evaluated with objective observation. Rightness is evaluated with judgment.

Creation must be the goal of goals. There is no joy in judgment. If you are constantly setting standards to achieve and judging yourself by those standards, you are stunting the amount of creativity that otherwise could have been utilized in the creation of the outcome you seek.

Take action! Not the kind of action that requires knowing that it is the right thing to do. No, because what happens when new information presents itself and you then become aware that you weren't "right" in the action you took. Now you judge yourself and your ability to know the right thing to do and become paralyzed with fear and reinforce doubt about yourself.

Certainty is the state of mind to have when you line up to the ball to create contact with it. There is no doubt in certainty, nor indeed can there be. Doubt doesn't relate to certainty, it relates to belief and since belief is not required, there is either certainty or there isn't.

Conversation with self while standing over the ball:

"I am going to hit this putt."

"But what if I have it lined up wrong? What if I don't strike it well? Then I'll miss it and I won't get a good score on this hole. Then I will be sure that I'm not a good golfer. Then I'll be worth less as a human."

Let's stop before any of this conversation takes place.

Instead, we'll just line up to the ball the way we want to. And with certainty, bring all our focus, attention, AND LOVE to the creation of contact between a spot on the ball and a spot on the face of the putter.

Leave the self-talk out. Enjoy the contact. Enjoy the certainty with which you take that action. It feels good. That is where the joy lies.

"Acting coaches in Hollywood were always telling me to use my hands and body more. But that was never me. I just breathe and sometimes it doesn't look as if I'm doing that."

Perry Como

Chapter 18

Moving the Baseline

As I have become more acutely aware of tension in my golf game, I have also become more acutely aware of the role that tension plays in my life.

I have realized that prior to The Epiphany, I walked around with a level of anxiety and fear that controlled how much fun I could have, how much I accomplished, and basically every other thing in my life. And I didn't even know it was there.

Since noticing it in my own life, I've observed the same type of existence in the lives of others, and discovered again that I am not nearly as unique as I once thought I was.

The truth is, we all become accustomed to a level of tension in our lives and over the course of time, we become completely immune to the fact that we're even feeling it. It just is.

Of course, it isn't necessary to live with this tension, but the possibility of living free of mental, emotional, and physical tension doesn't occur to most of us. It would likely not have occurred to me, either, had I not experienced The Epiphany.

I now look at tension, or fear and anxiety, or whatever we wish to call it, as optional.

I have created a simple graph as a visual tool to help me measure my own tension and uptightness. I refer to it as "The Perry Como Measurement."

If you don't remember Perry Como, please look him up on YouTube. You will be better for having done it. He was one of the most relaxed people to ever saunter on this planet. He was a crooner from the age of the great crooners and hung around with guys like Frank Sinatra and Dean Martin. He was my personal favorite, and the person whose demeanor I most aspire to emulate.

His ability to live in a relaxed manner was almost comical. So comical, in fact, that comedy teams have done skits mocking it!

The skits are hilarious but the gift of relaxation is not. I envy it! I want it for myself! I don't know how much golf Perry played, but I'll bet he was good at it. He certainly could sing.

The "Perry Como Measurement" measures the relative tension that I experience in my life, with Perry being the lowest possible level of tension or uptightness to achieve and The Tasmanian Devil being the highest. By using these two as the standards, I get to bring two of my loves into one analogy! Cartoons and Crooners.

I have discussed several things in this book that will temporarily lower tension, such as meditation and the utilization of The Concept while playing golf.

The greater and more enjoyable goal, however, would be to have The Concept become foundational thinking, our operating system, so that we actually move the baseline of tension that we experience in life. Once the baseline is moved, our experience of life will change drastically!

Imagine a life where almost nothing was an emergency. Where everything would be ok. Where you got to choose whether or not you wanted to be upset by something! Welcome to Perry's world. It is available to you.

It all hinges on embracing The Concept. The simple process of focusing on Contact with all your love and energy forces all thoughts that create tension from your mind.

When this way of thinking becomes part of who you are as a golfer, it will flow throughout your life and impact every relationship you have.

Those you love will start to wonder what happened to the old you. After all, a relaxed person is much easier to be around than an uptight person.

Once again, it's time to apply the "I love this in others" test. You will rarely, if ever, hear someone say, "You know what I love about him? I just love how uptight he is! I've got to get some of that in my life!"

There are a few bits of knowledge that I wish to pass along that can help move the baseline lower to produce a more tension-free and enjoyable life.

- If you are aware of why fear is present, then it can be replaced.
- You can change your world one round of golf at a time!
- Change occurs by degrees. Impatience is the enemy of real change.
- Discomfort is evidence of your mind clinging to a perceived truth and resisting new experience.
- Sincerely hoping for and celebrating the success of others frees the spirit!

This short list just scratches the service of the awarenesses that can be created to lower your baseline of tension. In my coaching, I help my clients find the things that work for them. The process can be very fun and rewarding in itself!

The Alternative

There is an alternative to embracing The Concept and it may be just fine for you to choose it. You may enjoy it. You may love having a lot of drama in your life. I know that sometimes, I crave drama.

My invitation is to recognize with a high level of awareness that it is a choice.

It is equally important to understand that how you are hitting the ball — or not hitting it — is purely based in choice.

You may feel as though it's something you just naturally can or can't do, but practicing with choice will show you that not only is that belief not true, but holding onto it does not help you in any way.

What I have discovered in looking back on my years of golf with much more objectivity than I could ever do prior to The Epiphany, is that I was a victim to my thoughts when it came to my relationship with golf.

Carrying tension, getting frustrated on the golf course, being a victim of my thoughts, and all other similar experiences are evidence that my baseline is closer to The Tasmanian Devil than it is to Perry on The Perry Como Measurement.

In my personal opinion, Perry is a better choice.

"WHAT LIES BEHIND US AND WHAT LIES BEFORE US ARE TINY MATTERS COMPARED TO WHAT LIES WITHIN US."

RALPH WALDO EMERSON

Chapter 19

The 19ᵗʰ Hole; What is YOUR Contact?

This is the question I invite you to ask yourself.

"What IS "Contact" for ME?"

Isn't golf fantastic? It gives such a clear visual about how instantaneous a moment actually is. Contact comes and goes in an instant!

Often, programs dealing with psychology and personal development will invite you to "be in the moment." This is an extremely valuable invitation and, if followed, can and will produce excellent results for you — if you can just come to an understanding of what a moment actually is and then learn how to be "in it!"

How can you be "in the moment?" The most effective way is to be AWARE of when you are out of it!

The question then becomes, "What is it that takes me OUT of the moment?" We have already discussed several possible answers to this question, which include concern for the future, dissatisfaction with past, fear that I'm not good enough, and any other number of thoughts.

There's value in recognizing these things, but far greater value in recognizing the TRUE root of what is taking you out of the moment.

If you go through your answers honestly and ask why to each one of them, you will inevitably take yourself deeper until you arrive at this answer: "I am concerned what others think of me." Before you dismiss this, as most people do when they first have it presented to them, search yourself honestly.

Do you REALLY want to change anything about the results you produce for yourself? If the answer to that question is YES, then you will do yourself no good by being in any way dishonest with yourself in the pursuit of understanding what it is that keeps you from any specific result.

You are in the moment when *your mind is completely free from anything unrelated to the connection with that instant you are experiencing.* Complete detachment from all things past and future allows complete presence in the moment.

The Concept is about understanding what a moment truly is. It is as small as that instant the clubface contacts the ball.

When I first experienced this Epiphany and clearly defined for myself what I now refer to as The Concept, I honestly thought it was useful only for golf.

I could not have been MORE wrong.

I was so excited about what was occurring with my game and with the experience of golf for me that I became overwhelmed with an enthusiasm to share it with a few of my friends and family to see how it would help them.

As had been the case with many things I had been excited about in the past, I anticipated a positive reception from some and a not as positive reception from others.

What actually happened was inspiring! I found that I received positive feedback and responses from everyone I shared The Concept with!

Not only that, I found that many of my golfing friends started to ask me questions about how to apply The Concept, and if I would be willing to coach them in it. I gladly shared what I could and watched as love for the game of golf returned to the lives of several of my friends who had also been on the verge of leaving it.

As time went on, I began to notice that The Concept was flowing out into other areas of my life.

First, it was tennis.

One day, I was playing tennis with a friend of mine who typically beats me pretty soundly. And by typically, I mean he had beaten me basically every time we'd played in the previous six months! Anyway, I was down 3-2 in the first set and getting very frustrated with my play when it occurred to me that The Concept is equally as applicable to tennis as it is to golf. It might be, if for no other reason than for the sake of enjoyment, worth my while to utilize it here!

I decided that I would watch the ball as I tossed it on the serve and just be aware of exactly how the racquet was contacting it. That required a visual focus, really seeing the ball get contacted by the racquet strings, and a heightened awareness of the "feeling" of the strings striking or brushing the ball.

I decided also that I would remain focused on the ball as it was struck back to me and then bring as much love and attention to contacting it with my groundstrokes and volleys. Well, I did lose another game, but that was all I lost as I went on to win 6-4, 6-0.

How did that happen? Can a simple change of mindset really create an outcome that drastically different?

That friend's name is Mark and he is a great friend. He has been a sounding board throughout this discovery and has helped me refine and implement The Concept. He was the first person to point out that The Concept could be universal in its application and asked me to please teach it to his manager at work! The tension created by focusing on results was absolutely killing morale in the office.

We successfully applied it to our tennis and went from mediocre players who seldom had a rally beyond five shots to senior-tour versions of Nadal and Federer, blasting rallies of twenty or thirty shots or more. The greatest part about all of this is that our enjoyment of the game of tennis has skyrocketed!

Ok. So now I was certain The Concept worked for sports, but what about other things?

The next thing it really started to impact for me was singing.

For many years, I have been involved in some very high-level theatrical and musical productions and have found great enjoyment participating in them.

I've played such roles as Javert in *Les Miserables* and Sweeney in *Sweeney Todd* as well as a variety of roles in opera and straight theater. I have also had the opportunity to tour around much of the world with some tremendous choral organizations performing beautiful music.

The common theme for me over those 20 plus years of performance is that I always had tension around my voice. Lots of tension. As a matter of fact, I had practiced and performed singing incorrectly for so many years that it had become extremely difficult for me to allow any of the muscles associated with singing to relax in a way that made singing enjoyable for me.

Here was one more thing I seemed to be fairly decent at but didn't really love because it was so incredibly hard for me!

I even went to a world-renowned voice teacher who is so exclusive that people fly in from all around the United States just for voice lessons!

She listened to me sing and then gave me some very direct feedback. "Basically," she said, "you have a beautiful instrument, but everything you do technically is wrong." I find it somewhat humorous to look at all I've accomplished with singing, considering the fact that I have done it mostly incorrectly!

But in the last two years, something amazing has happened! I have learned to focus on the feeling of singing rather than judging myself (and thereby creating wretched tension) by the sound I produce.

The "Contact" in singing is the moment breath passes over the vocal chords and makes them vibrate and produce a sound. I am learning to love that event and the feeling around it rather than judging myself on what hits my ears.

As a matter of fact, as I mentioned in Chapter 10, I now practice with my ears plugged or covered so that I can't hear myself! It's the singing equivalent of the "no-target" practice I do while on the driving range.

What I hear when I sing isn't what I actually sound like, anyway.

My love for singing is now greater than it has ever been and my ability to do it is improving on a daily basis, as The

Concept becomes my foundation. Now, I even incorporate singing nearly every time I speak to groups.

Look at what you do. What are you passionate about? What do you teach?

What is YOUR Contact?

It could be anything.

My daughter, Jaci, is a professional photographer. She has been obsessed with photography since she was 14 and has become somewhat famous because she is so good at it.

Photography, maybe more than any other activity or skill, is dependent upon the photographer bringing focus and love to what they are doing. It is all about capturing moments. And not just capturing moments, but helping to create them!

Jaci used to offer photo shoots for anyone who wanted them so that she could get better at her craft. My computer is as slow as molasses because of the hundreds of thousands of photos I still have from her practice shoots!

Contact occurs for her when she captures an image of the model she's shooting that connects with those who see it. She brings so much love and focus to her photography that she is regularly able to see things in others they can't even see in themselves, and she shares those things through her art. She LOVES what she does and she is an expert at it!

When I speak to groups, Contact for me is connecting with those I am speaking to. I want to experience them. I want to see what is coming up for them. I want to find the way to share my message with them that they will understand. Connecting with other human beings is the ultimate Contact!

What is YOUR CONTACT? What in your life can you bring all your love to? Can you let go of the tension that you may now have related to worry and attachment to outcome and results?

What would you like to enjoy more than you do now? What do you want to be better at and have more fun with? Where is the tension in your life that is sabotaging you from experiencing and having what you want?

Where is the source of tension that's holding you back from BEING who you want to be? Find the Why beneath the Why until you have been completely honest with yourself and gone as far as you can go. Then let The Concept work for you.

Right now, while you are reading this, something is coming up for you. Sit with it. Write it down. What is the most direct action you can take out of love right now, completely absent of attachment to outcome or fear of the past?

Choose to do it. The rewards are magnificent!

Why Capture My Message in a Book?
(A short commentary on writing)

Why do we write?

We write to express things that can't be held inside of us. We write because the solitude and meditative nature of writing promotes clarity of thought and therapy to the spirit.

Modern society, driven by marketing and the belief that money is the only way to assign value to something, would say that we write books because doing so makes us more marketable.

That may be partly true, but PLEASE do not let it be the reason you write a book! If it is, both you and your book will suffer for it!

We write books because our souls cannot rest until we do.

The transfer of thought to physical manifestation challenges us to become so clear in our certainty that it actually changes the way we live. The writing of our message helps us to become it.

Writing is also an amazing way to share your passions and certainties with others, because it is free from the contamination of conventional social delivery systems.

Why are books and other sources of media — particularly written — such an effective means of communication of ideas? It is mostly because the reader, in the solitude of their consumption of the media, is more open to the ideas and thoughts being conveyed than they ever would be through conversation.

In human interaction, we are susceptible to the "Argue or Withdraw" mechanism, which is my modern-day emotional equivalent to the "Fight or Flight" mechanism. (If you would like it to be cool sounding and rhyme like the other one, you may also refer to it as the "Cry or Fly" mechanism!)

In social settings, all but the truly peaceful are guarded against possible exposure that they may be perceived as unintelligent, uninformed, less than enough, or just flat out wrong.

Oh, the horror of such possibilities!

Of course they are guarded! It is human nature to protect oneself!

The difference is that we no longer have to run from a saber-toothed tiger to protect our physical lives. No. The present-day beast we run from is the emotional discomfort of feeling that others don't approve of us!

Books can break through this barrier or actually sidestep it altogether!

When the social possibility of being made wrong is eliminated, consumers will find themselves seeking truth or resonance inside of the media they are engaged with.

They will look for things they agree with or, even better, just let what they read settle on their minds like a soft snowfall.

Not only that, but by buying your book and taking it home to enjoy in the quiet, peaceful comfort of their own home they have given you permission to share any and all of your ideas with them. You are in!

The power of the inside-invite is not limited to just vampires!

Please write! Put your message on paper (or Kindle!) and watch and experience the power of it grow within you!

It took me three years to write this book. Well, three months to write it and 33 months to wallow in fear ABOUT writing it.

What was I afraid of? Eventually, I figured it out and when my own message permeated me to the point where I truly got it, I wrote.

The very thing that has held me back from letting this book out into the world is what keeps people from embracing The Concept.

It is too simple.

We want to be clever. We want to come up with something new and exciting. We want to be able to say that what we are saying is different.

Well, here's the truth of it. If what we are saying is simple, then it is different. Everyone wants to appear smart. There is no pride in saying that you comprehend something that anyone down to a five-year-old could comprehend.

That is the beauty of ideas that really take hold and make a difference in the lives of those that embrace them. They are simple. They are easy to embody. They go against the masses.

In *Inception*, one of my favorite movies, the main character (played by Leonardo DiCaprio) is charged with the task of planting an idea deep in the subject's subconscious while in a dream state, which will ultimately change everything about that person.

For *Inception* to work effectively, the subject must believe that the idea originated with him. Why? Because if he thinks someone else planted the idea there, he will reject it out of natural human defensiveness.

Humans do not like being told what to do or think.

We do, however, love to have options that elevate, inspire, relieve fear and tension, and generate feelings of happiness and well-being. Options that we choose ourselves. Options that become visible to us when our foundational thinking allows them to.

The greatest idea is the one that heightens awareness, diminishes judgment, fosters clarity, and creates connection to spirit.

My strongest invitation is that we use this gift of inception to plant deep within ourselves, even at our very foundational level of thought, The Concept, or whatever we may choose to call it, so that all that is experienced by us is experienced through its lens.

Let us be so focused on and in love with the passion that we are invested in at the moment, so as to experience the greatest joy possible!

Through my passion for golf, I learned a way to bring love into the instantaneous, present moment, so that I was free of fear, doubt, worry, and tension!

Remember that tension in the present moment sabotages all the great things that moment otherwise could have provided.

Let's raise our glasses to enjoying life more than we ever imagined possible. Let us toast to experiencing more fearless success! To having deeper, more connected relationships that fill our souls with joy and resonate to the center of our beings!

Let us connect. Let us love.

What is YOUR CONTACT?

Please remember:

The Concept is this:

The only thing that matters is **CONTACT**.

LOVE THE CREATION OF THAT CONNECTION UNCONDITIONALLY and everything else will take care of itself.

Why does The Concept work? It works because...

Fear and doubt about the past (no matter how recent) combined with worry about and attachment to some desired future outcome create TENSION in the moment and sabotage nearly all chance of that desired future outcome occurring.

Please send your questions and feedback to:

andrew@whatsmycontact.com

About the Author

Andrew McKee is a Speaker, AUTHOR, and Coach whose greatest joy and happiness is found with his wife and three children. And since I am Andrew McKee and I am writing this about myself, I will continue this short narrative in first person.

I LOVE human connection. I love being able to communicate and associate with people. I think people are the greatest thing this planet has to offer.

I LOVE golf. I love how much can be learned and experienced through playing golf. I love how participating in golf and other activities with an UNCOMMON LEVEL OF AWARENESS can teach us about relationships and how to make them more powerful and fulfilling than we may have ever imagined.

I LOVE speaking. I love listening to great speakers. I love and appreciate thought leaders who have invested so much of their lives seeking to understand people and how to best serve them. I have been curious about those things for most of my life and have invested thousands of hours seeking to understand why I and others think and act the way we do.

If you are interested in my education, work history and accomplishments, and other such things which I find less important than what I have included above, please contact me and I'll share those details with you.

andrew@whatsmycontact.com

Printed in Great Britain
by Amazon